CARL GORHAM

MY LIFE

in a

GARDEN

Love, loss and mulch:
a single dad seeks answers in nature

¶I Ireton Press

¶ Ireton Press

_____

First published in Great Britain in 2025

Copyright © Carl Gorham 2025

ISBN: 978-1-0686544-0-4

Printed and bound in Great Britain by Clays Ltd, Bungay plc.

Some names and details have been changed, some events
have been compressed and some dialogue has been recreated.
The rest is as I remember it.

carlgorham.com

@carlmgorham

For Romy, Emma, Ben and Lexy.

PREFACE

November 2020

The ageing widow pruning her roses, lost in memories of the love she has lost; the obsessive fanatic cutting his hedge with the precision of a Rodin sculpture; the young eco-conscious couple pulling turnips out of the ground as triumphantly as if they were buried Viking treasures; the hobbyist, the bored, the happy, the avoidant, the depressed – there are as many versions of the relationship between gardens and people as there are gardens and people.

This is the story of mine. How we were enemies. How we were friends. How I hated it. How I missed it. How I drew strength and support and understanding from it. How at times it seemed as if it were rebelling against me and trying to teach me something about my own stubbornness. How it made me cry. How it made me laugh. How I enjoyed its company. How it entertained and bewitched me. How I celebrated it. How I drew spiritual strength from it. How I once even used it as a pick-up line.

How we went through death, grief, illness and a break-down together. How we saw the best of times and the worst of times.

My garden was no ordinary place – it was a huge, three-acre sprawl with a maze and an orchard and a sunken dell. I was no ordinary gardener, either – I was an entirely useless one who, for various reasons, had to suddenly take up the role on a full-time basis.

We were possibly the most ill-matched pair in history, and our relationship was as volatile as you might expect – full of tiffs and anger, silent glares, tantrums and loathing; full of me swearing that I would really like to sell it, leave and never come back.

But in the end, I didn't, and I'm glad I didn't, because I wouldn't be the person I am today without it.

Now, as I look back over the last 15 years since we first met, I can see that in some ways it was one of the more substantial relationships I have had in that period, albeit a rather strange and twisted one. We, certainly in the last year, spent longer in each other's company than almost anyone else's. And even when we weren't together, I found myself thinking about it a lot.

I am surprised at how deep and intimate our relation-ship became. Many of my key moments have been played out in front of the garden, in it or next to it. Much emotion has been expended because of it; I don't seem to have kept much back from it or been shy of showing it my deepest secrets.

Preface

When I set out to write this book, I thought I was going to create something different and much simpler – an account of a specific project to transform an overgrown garden into something marketable despite my lack of gardening nous; an account of a fixed period, a few months in 2019, that explored a series of changes in my natural environment whilst mapping the effect it had on myself.

But life, not for the first time, proved more complicated. The more I wrote about that experience, the more it brought back other memories, echoes from the years preceding it: significant moments of pain, humour, frustration, awkwardness, bewilderment and delight; questions and answers; sometimes questions without answers. We are all of us living in the past as well as in the present, skipping back and forth, our lives a fragmentary, uneven patchwork of old hurts and anxieties, long-ago happiness and sorrows. It quickly became apparent that I couldn't truly represent today without dipping back into yesterday – to a degree that surprised even me.

I make no apologies for ending up in a different place than I expected. I have always believed that writing is a richly organic, surprising process, and that when it ceases to be that for the writer, it tends to be so for the reader as well. What I do know is that where I have ended up is as true an expression of my overall experience as I can muster.

So, if this book is about a specified few months in time, it is also about threads that have run through a lifetime.

It spreads out from the centre in many directions, like a tree has many branches, not all of them neat and well balanced; some are misshapen and untidy, many battered and scarred. It doesn't draw neat conclusions. It doesn't believe in fairytales.

If I were to try and sum up the book in neat, publisher-friendly speak, to summarise its themes of bereavement and nature and its blend of comedy and drama, I might struggle to come up with a pithy sentence; I might even fail to come up with a pithy paragraph.

Maybe the best option is just to keep it simple.

It's my life in a garden.

THE GARDEN

This is a map of the garden. If it looks a bit like the map that Tolkien had at the beginning of *The Hobbit*, that's because *The Hobbit* was one of the first books I was ever given and remains an inspiration to me as a writer.

It is also symbolic for as you will see, my plans to conquer the gardening world have been just as fraught with danger, difficulty, and embarrassment as Bilbo Baggins's attempts to get through the misty mountains and across the great plains beyond.

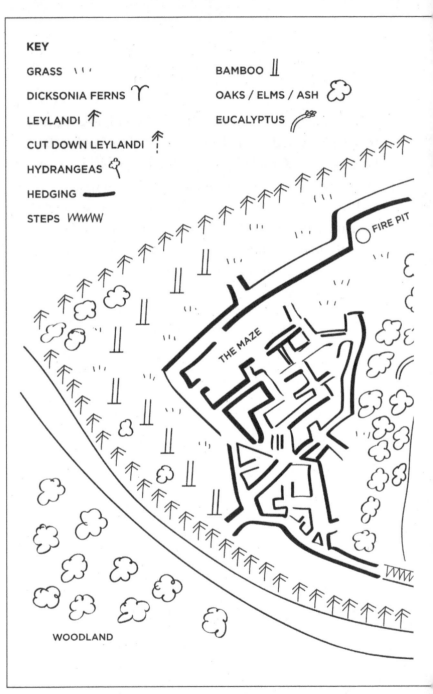

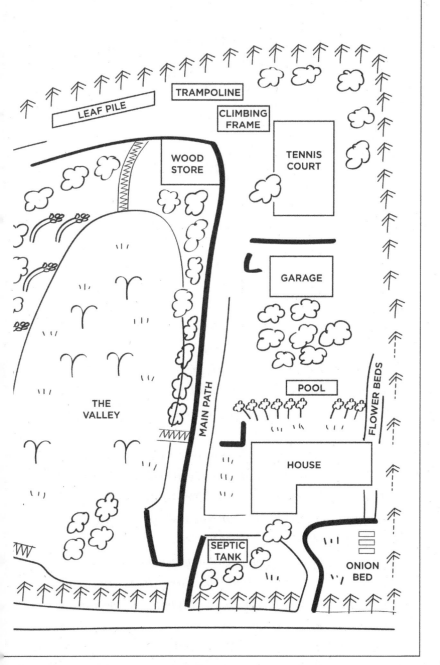

VERSAILLES

June 2005

My wife Vikki and I are looking out onto the garden of a house. It is a magnificent garden, like something from Versailles, and we may be about to buy it.

We are standing in a part of the garden we already call The Valley (we call it that the first time we see it and the name will stick forever afterwards – we much prefer it to the rather effete description in the estate agent's brochure, "sunken woodland dell"). The Valley is an old Victorian chalk quarry to the left-hand side of the house, beyond the long, straight, gravel path that leads up to the garage. You descend a rickety set of 16 steps and find yourself in a huge, flat, grassy area that is dotted with Dicksonia ferns and Gunnera – Day of the Triffids-*style plants with massive stems that reach up to the sky with, at their tips, huge leaves the size of frisbees.*

The grassy area is surrounded by steep banks on three sides that are at least fifty feet high; these are filled with shrubs, flowers and trees – elm, ash and eucalyptus. On these banks there are also other paths that wind their way out of The Valley and, in a couple of places, high up, are wooden seats tucked into the undergrowth, where you can sit and contemplate the magnificent view.

Time just seems to melt away when you are in The Valley. You are overtaken by the scale of it – suddenly you feel tiny in comparison to the huge banks and massive plants, the towering trees and gigantic palms.

There is little noise in this vast natural bowl; the outside world is kept at bay. All you hear is the rustling of the wind through the undergrowth, a sound that swells and then fades with a massive russshhhh. As soon as the sound disappears, it begins again, so it is impossible to tell when one sound has started and the other ended – a constant swirling hiss, as if you were standing in the middle of the sea.

In The Valley, life slows, simplifies, and you can hear your own thoughts; you can take them out and re-examine them and put them back. It is utterly magical. It isn't just a garden, it's an experience – the kind of place you might normally expect to find in Kew Gardens or Alice in Wonderland; the kind of place you take pictures of, the kind of place that makes you say "Wow!" out loud the first time you see it.

The Valley is the thing we talk about when we leave that afternoon. It is the thing that stays with us in the coming days and weeks. In many ways, it is the thing that will lead us to buy this house and this garden – not that there aren't other amazing things to look at, there are many. The Valley is just one part of an extraordinary plot.

At the front is a curved drive that leads down to the road. On one side of the drive as you enter is a majestic lawn with some raised beds and apple trees. On the other side of the drive is another lawn with several beds containing shrubs and tall elms. Along the edge of the garden, where it meets the road, is a line of towering Leylandii conifers. Because the main drive is curved, the house is almost completely invisible to passers-by.

There is another triangular patch of grass at the back of the house, next to the kitchen. Here you can eat breakfast at a table that sits on a gravelled section, with a riotous bank of gorgeous hydrangeas behind it.

In one corner are steps up that lead you through to another grassy area, where there is an outdoor swimming pool (our own swimming pool!) surrounded by a patio, and further on from there is another huge, flat, open area of grass where there is a sizeable climbing frame and a grass tennis court (our own tennis court!).

Beyond that, as you curve round to the left, skirting the top end of The Valley, is a whole new section of garden, uneven and grassy, that slopes gently down to the hedge that runs along its base, parallel to the road. Here, there is a copper-beech maze (our own maze!) with long, twisting avenues of hedging that veer left and right and at times seem to double back on themselves (I have now lived with it for ten years and still get lost).

Within the maze are several hidden, enclosed circular areas with beds of grasses and bamboo plants – wonderful little kingdoms that you only stumble upon as you try to grope your way out of the confusing network of tunnels and cul-de-sacs. Once you are through the maze, you find a path that leads down into the other side of The Valley, which you can cross, then climb back up to the house.

The house itself is impressive – a vast warren of good-size rooms with bedrooms galore and a playroom and a kitchen and separate dining room, plus a huge hallway with a spectacular butterfly staircase; even a music room.

When we first see the house, it appears oddly grown-up – the kind of place your parents might like, with carpets everywhere, Artex ceilings and framed maps all over the walls, but the dimensions of the place are impressive and the potential clearly immense.

By the time we have seen the house and garden and are standing once more at the bottom of The Valley, gazing up at the vast banks of greenery on either side, we are head-over-heels in love with the place, and partly in shock, too. We have a tiny, terraced house in London, a two-up, two-down with a thirty-foot garden, and in the crazy world of house prices, it seems, with a little juggling and a small mortgage here or there, we can basically swap one for the other.

Vikki looks at me. Her eyes are dancing with excitement. Her smile is irrepressible and wide as The Valley itself.

We can give our four-year-old daughter Romy everything she would ever want and more, a dream outdoor existence where she can run free with her friends away from cars and buses and pollution. Camping. Swimming. Tennis. Roasting marshmallows under the stars. The greatest games of hide-and-seek. Swallows and Amazons.

We can grow things and we can eat healthily. With a garden this size we could even open our own shop. We can have friends round and play loud music if we want. We can party and celebrate, or we can just sit in the glorious Valley and let that incredible rushing breeze blow our cares away.

There is another motivation, too, a massive force like a hurricane that is driving us onwards. Vikki has just come out of cancer treatment. The future is uncertain. We are running now, grabbing at life before it slips through our fingers. We are desperate for experience, for opportunity. We want to taste everything before it's maybe too late. And now this once-in-a-lifetime possibility has arisen, just dropped in our laps. A golden, shining prize. A whole new life wrapped up in three acres of stunning greenery. Surely this is serendipity. Surely this is meant to be.

"Let's just do it," she says, looking at me.

Now she has spoken, it's as if it has already happened. As if we have already taken possession of this huge estate and leapt forwards in time. As if we are now surveying our own kingdom.

I feel giddy with the sheer speed of it. Elated. As if we are flying. Fast, very fast. Hurtling.

I feel a sudden panic, too. That I can't stop. That we can't stop. That we are rushing into something too big.

How are we going to keep up the garden? We won't have the money left over to get a full-time gardener. Christ, it would take an army of gardeners to deal with this place. It would take a residential army of gardeners. This is madness. Vikki has just finished two years of cancer treatment. The future is a road that quickly falls away from us, one where we can't see what is coming up. Look at the beds, the neatly mown lawns, the tidy edges, the well-pruned shrubs. I know nothing about gardening. This is such a huge undertaking. Serendipity? This is crazy.

"Shall we?" she says, smiling at me.

"Of course," I say. "Of course."

November 2018

I am standing in roughly the same spot as before in The Valley with my new partner, Emma.

Except it is not the same at all.

Where before there were the huge *Day of the Triffids*-style plants, there are now just brown stumps, and the giant Gunnera are withered and sit miserably on the ground, their leaves crushed and limp.

Both sides of The Valley are overgrown with nettles that almost obscure the plants; they are also pockmarked with rabbit and other animal holes. Indeed, there are so many that there has been some erosion, and great chunks of earth have slipped down and now lie in piles on the edge of the grass.

We have just done a circuit of the whole garden and have already seen the overgrown beds on the front lawn – the lawn itself riddled with moss, the beds full of weeds and tatty at the edges.

Outside the kitchen windows, the bank of hydrangeas has grown out and over the edge of the lawn, almost engulfing one end of the outdoor table, the deadheads of the flowers in dire need of pruning as they bob lifelessly in the wind.

The patio round the swimming pool is beset by weeds, and the tennis court at the top is more moss than grass, with divots where rabbits and squirrels have been at work. The maze is untidy; many of the avenues of beech hedging have grown over and are now impassable.

The main path that leads up from the road between the pool and The Valley is matted with weeds, and there is a carpet of green lichen over some of it, especially the long, straight section that leads up to the garage, where it is turning into a lawn, albeit an ugly one with stones in.

All the hedges are unkempt and straggly, like a tramp's beard, and none of the individual shrubs have been shaped or pruned in a while, so those hedges next to the house are obliterating the views from the windows, and those around the garden have just spread out and grown into one another, like gangly teenage lovebirds entwined on a sofa.

The whole garden looks like a tatty portrait of itself in need of restoration, one where chunks of paint have been chipped off, where the colours have faded in the light and the definition of the lines has become blurred. You can tell that it used to be very fine once, but that was obviously a very long time ago. It looks tired and careworn – much like its owner.

A lot has happened to the garden since 2005.

A lot has happened to me, too.

Vikki died in 2007, while we were abroad on a family holiday to Australia. Unbeknown to us, her cancer, which she'd seemingly defeated, had come back, more virulent and uncontrollable than ever. She collapsed on the return flight from a holiday in Sydney, was too ill to continue her journey after the stopover in Hong Kong and died there two weeks later.

Nothing prepares you for losing someone, and even though we had lived with that possibility for so long it still felt like a seismic shock. I was devastated, as was Romy.

I kept the house and garden when we got back. That seemed important, as if by doing so, we were keeping a part of Vikki alive. She had loved it so much, she had wanted it so much, I just didn't want to sell up. It didn't feel right. I wanted to hold on to it because I wanted to hold on to her. I wanted to make her dream happen; I wanted to honour her memory and use it to help make more of our own.

I didn't want to disrupt things for Romy, either. There'd been enough disruption already. I wanted to keep things rooted. Grounded. Familiar. We'd only just moved in when the tragedy happened; the thought of moving yet again seemed crazy.

So I kept it. I kept it all. From 2007 to the present day, 11 years later.

I kept it all, despite the garden slowly falling apart. Despite the hedges mutating into giant, unkept walls. Despite the nettles growing in, around and over everything like greedy, inquisitive neighbours. Despite the trees growing unchecked and dwarfing the house. Despite the beds becoming overgrown and the path being eaten by moss. Even though I knew that every time I got on the ride-on lawnmower and whizzed round, I was fighting a losing battle; that in a way, it was a kind of tragic, futile gesture.

It is not a complete wasteland, of course. There is still greenery and beds, and you can tell where one sort of ends and the other sort of begins, and there are big shrubs and huge trees, and sometimes, at first glance, it is so impressive in scope you miss some of the awkward detail. But I know the truth; I know what is there – the kind of mess it has become.

Now, as I look at it with my new partner, Emma, it is time to move on.

I can no longer afford this house and garden, with their capacity to just eat through money. I can no longer afford to pump the water round the pool. I can no longer afford to heat the many rooms. I can no longer afford to keep it clean or to replace the window frames, which have needed renewing for a while. Or to patch up the roof, which is always leaking.

Recently we found a perfect, much smaller home nearby with a sensible-sized one-hundred-foot garden, thinking we would move in together and share resources (Emma still had a house of her own nearby). She managed to sell hers, which was enough, along with a sizeable mortgage, to finance the move. The only fly in the ointment was that we couldn't sell mine.

Increasing Brexit uncertainty froze the local market into an iceberg. We changed estate agents after six months, hoping to change our fortunes, but after several weeks on the market with the new agency, we hadn't had a single viewing. We started to panic – the costs of the new place and just keeping the old house going were beginning to spiral out of control. Bills piled up. Money flowed out like water. My work as a TV writer chose this crucial time to start drying up completely.

So, for the time being, we have taken my house off the market, and we are now about to let out it out as a holiday rental to help cover costs and provide some much-needed income.

It seems a sensible, pragmatic option. Emma has experience of the hotel business, having been brought up in one and worked in several when she was younger. She is going to take on responsibility for the house, while I have been given the job of sorting out the garden.

There is just one problem with this whole well-thought-out idea.

I am the world's most useless gardener.

PARTY

May 2007

I am sinking in grief. Vikki died a month ago and I am still almost unable to say those words. If I try, they choke me, like hands around my throat.

I exist in a strange world of foggy bewilderment and disbelief, floating and confused. Time rushes by and stands still all at once. I am manic and paralysed. I have energy and I'm exhausted. Through it all, some sort of life goes on, though I don't know how.

I pull my aching, tremulous body through the days by making lists of things to do and following them as if they were the Ten Commandments. The business of estate, a memorial service and Romy's return to school all happen, but after each of these events it feels as if I couldn't possibly have been there, and a ghost has taken my place.

Romy's birthday party, originally scheduled for the end of April, was cancelled because we were in Hong Kong and dealing with darker, more pressing issues, such as which sort of coffin to choose for Vikki's repatriation. Now, a month after that traumatic trip, it feels imperative to do it, despite Vikki's death.

Because of Vikki's death.

It feels important not just to do it, but to do it well. Really well. It must be the best party ever. It must be the most glorious, the most colourful, the most unexpected, the funniest, most dramatic, most exciting six-year-old's party in history.

It matters so much. Everything matters so much. In these raw, early days when I am still clutching at life through desperate fingers, everything feels like a tribute to Vikki; something that must be fitting; something that must be appropriate; something that must measure up; something that must represent her and all she meant.

I am building statues to her every minute of the day.

A witch from Norwich has turned up in a Vauxhall Corsa and will provide the entertainment. Vikki booked her months ago and I find myself almost immediately floored by a wave of grief when she arrives and presents me with her signed contract which has, at the bottom of the page, my late wife's signature. At least the witch looks the part, with her pointy hat, black outfit and broomstick; she even has a scary-looking cat taped to her shoulder.

A grumpy local man with tattoos the size of shop signs has provided the marquee where she will cast her spells and where we will eat if it rains. We have set it up on the tennis court at the top of the garden so that the entire afternoon can be spent outdoors.

Party

The location of the party is no accident. It feels important to use the garden for this – to make use of its size and scale. I want the kids to have space and run around and exhaust themselves. I want them to enjoy the freedom. This was what Vikki had spoken of when we stood in The Valley before we bought it, and I can hear her words in my head now, clanging like church bells. The garden as a place to hold special events, to make memories. A wonderland. Versailles. Swallows and Amazons.

I wait nervously as the first kids arrive (they are at an age where the parents will stay for the duration of the party). My stomach is rolled as tight as a bowling ball and my voice sounds thin and cartoon-like, as if I've just inhaled from one of the helium balloons I've attached to the trellis around the tennis court. The idea is that I will meet and greet at the house, then send them all up the path that leads to the play area at the top. My sister-in-law will be waiting for them there, along with the witch, who has told me she will start her performance as soon as they arrive.

So I wait, and I greet, and I'm aware of my own manic behaviour by this time, my charged-up, adrenaline-fuelled facial expressions, the ridiculous clown's smile, my huge hand gestures and my too-loud voice, but I can't seem to dial down my own craziness. In fact, it only seems to be increasing, as if someone has plugged my body into a new and vibrant power source. As they arrive, I shout and make great swooping gestures, firing my arm out like an arrow towards the marquee and bellowing, "PARTY UP THAT WAY!" Then, when the last of Romy's friends arrives, I shut the back door of the house and follow them up the path to the party that I pray is in full swing and totally bewitched, terrified and spellbound by the woman with the cat on her shoulder – the darkest, most devilish witch who ever left Norwich in a Vauxhall Corsa.

Except it isn't. At all.

The party isn't in full swing. It is as if it's finished.

Instead of shouting spells and waving her wand, instead of sending the kids scuttling for cover and yelling "Arrgghh"; instead of being a proper, scary ghoul, the witch is muttering something inaudible into a microphone as if she is going through her expenses claim for the booking. The kids who are sitting around her feet in a semi-circle look bored as hell. Others have already wandered off. Some are talking. The parents, meanwhile, look on, unimpressed. One or two of them have resorted to gossiping. Another is playing on their daughter's Nintendo DS.

Romy's birthday party, the one that had to be postponed because of her mother's death, the one that her mother had planned so carefully, the one that her mother would have wanted to be as perfect as possible, is a disaster.

A disaster presided over by me.

I run up to the witch from Norwich and snatch the mic out of her hand (what is surprising in retrospect is how little she seems to resist – she almost seems grateful). Then I yell, "RIGHT, LISTEN, EVERYONE!" so loudly it nearly blows the mic apart. All the kids stop because the sound of my voice is so harsh and grating, like someone grinding metal, and I know I must look strange, my face red, my eyes popping out like giant, bloodshot footballs, but I can't stop, I just daren't stop. So I bellow, "LISTEN!" which again nearly blows the mic out of my hands, and I start doing some insane, jumpy little step like the creatures on the Yellow Brick Road in The Wizard of Oz. *I have no idea what the hell I am doing; all I know is I must do something to get their attention.*

"MUSICAL STATUES, YEEEAAAHHHHHHHHHH!"

We don't have any music set up, so I start doing the music myself. "LA-LA-LA-LA-LA-LA-LA…"

Then I shout, "STOP!"

And they all freeze, but one wobbles, so I point at him. "YOU!" He sits down with a rueful look, disappointed to be out of the game.

The shouting recommences. "AGAIN!!!!!! LALALALALALALALALALALA!!!!"

I remember, years ago, when I did an open spot as a standup comedian in the notorious Tunnel Club, located just outside the Blackwall Tunnel in South London (they used to throw ashtrays at an act if they didn't like them). I was doing a double act with my then comic partner Amanda Swift and we were so petrified, we did a 20-minute act in five minutes. And that is exactly what I think of now, here, as I yell and sweat and leave no gaps for the audience to heckle me off stage, or say they are bored, or ask if they can go home because the party is rubbish.

We do all the games I can think of, and when I have run out of normal games, I just do messy, charging-around games that aren't proper party games, like British Bulldog and Piggyback

Rides. Then I eventually run out of even those games and start doing one I have just invented called "EVERYONE JUMP ON ROMY'S DAD!"

And they literally pile on me and I just bellow, "Agh! Oh! Eugh!" and "Ow!!" into the mic as they leap and dive on top of me in a mad, writhing, squealing mass.

Then, when I can't think of anything else to do, even some stupid game I've thought up, I just bellow anything that comes into my head.

"LET'S ALL POGO!"

"STICK YOUR LEGS IN THE AIR!"

"MAKE FARTY NOISES!"

Some of the parents are looking on faintly alarmed; even the ones who are smiling look like it's been fixed on with superglue, but I can't stop. I've gone too far, been taken over by the spirit of someone else, by this crazed person, and I jump up and down and wipe away the dribble from my mouth as I jump because I am just salivating with the effort and I can feel the blood pumping through my neck and the sweat pouring down the back of my shirt.

I look at my watch.

Ten minutes have passed.

Christ. Is that all?

From nowhere, I just start shouting, "FORM A LINE!"

Not because I know what I'm doing, but because I just have to fill the air with noise. The kids quickly get in line because it is what they are programmed to do, and it eats up a precious few seconds but no more, and soon they are looking at me for the next instruction, the next instruction that I don't have.

"COMPANY! MARCH!" suddenly comes to me, I don't know where from. I find myself quoting Colonel Hathi from The Jungle Book *and his booming voice and I lead them off, with exaggerated elephantine strides, swinging my arms up and down like piston rods, raising my feet imperiously and stamping them into the ground. I lead them out of the tennis court area and round the climbing frame and the trampoline, again and again. Then, conscious of the need for something different, I turn right by the giant oak tree into the area which houses the maze.*

Down the path we go, through the wooden arbour at the entrance, straight into a tunnel with high hedges on both sides that leads to a little crossroads where three other paths meet the one we are on. I lead them right, along the widest of the avenues, and find myself feeling relieved and grateful for the space that just seems to open for me now, which goes on forever with the bright sky above as hard as a sheet of metal and the hedges on either side a long green wall, seemingly without beginning and end.

On and on we go, further and further, away from the tennis court and the marquee and the memories of a party that was failing, down the avenue, looping back up another, in our own party now, with everyone in time or their own shambolic version of time; marching, yelling, laughing, passing other beech-lined paths that shoot off in different directions.

I don't remember the maze being like this – this complicated, this magnificent. It is certainly bigger than I recall, probably because the kids are small, but whatever the reason, the maze seems to tower over us now, engulf us, pick us up and put us down somewhere different, in a place that is almost overpowering, that reeks of damp leaves and fresh grass, of lush moss and wet bark. It feels as if we have come miles, not yards, the sense of isolation as keen and exciting and exotic as if we had stumbled on a Pacific Island.

Party

I sense a change in the kids almost immediately. They seem intrigued by the new space around them; less restless, less trapped in their own irrepressibly energetic bodies, more focussed on the outside, on the gorgeous backdrop and the mysterious journey that I am leading them on. Already one or two of them are racing off the back of my column and disappearing down other avenues, calling out to those still in line who can hear them but can't see them, then suddenly jumping back out to surprise them.

We keep weaving round the maze along the paths, with me still barking commands but with a less noticeable swish through the long grass behind me now, as more and more of them join in this impromptu game of 'now you see me, now you don't'. Eventually, on the fourth circuit of the maze, I stop and turn, and the last in the line take this as a signal to peel off, run back and join their friends.

As I walk back alone, I see the kids are now happily amused without me, darting in and out of the hedge-lined avenues, disappearing into the spaces between. They have formed themselves into teams and are taking it in turns to melt into the undergrowth and then be sought out by the others.

The game is a fast, energetic one, the maze a blur of rushing, small bodies that flit in and out of sight like colourful versions of the muntjac deer that appear in the maze from time to time, the soundtrack a continuous bubbling soup of high-pitched shrieks, sharp whispers and triumphant exclamations.

I watch all this from the bottom of one of the beech avenues, near where the maze rolls down to the steps that lead into

The Valley. From there, I can look back up the longest straight avenue and see the action along adjoining paths. I am now just an observer, neither in control nor needed, and delighted with both developments. I can enjoy the sight of the maze and its new habitants; I can delight in the fact that the maze is providing exactly what is needed. For the first time the party is running itself.

I look at my watch again.

Nearly half an hour has gone.

I am safe.

Time for tea.

We reassemble the line and come back out of the maze again, back round the trampoline and the climbing frame and into the tennis court area where the marquee is and where the parents are still grouped. I wave to my sister-in-law, and she brings out the plates of marshmallows and crisps and sausage rolls and cheese straws and rolls that have been hidden away behind the marquee. I shout, "TEEEAAAA!" and I can barely get the word out because I am losing my voice. As the kids crowd round the plates like ants, I see that in the corner the witch is already halfway through a sausage roll.

A weird silence descends, as it does whenever kids are stuffing their faces and they don't need entertaining, and all you can hear is a lot of low breathing and feverish chomping. My body is feeling really tired now, aching, finally letting go of all that angst, that anticipation. I know that when the food is finished, it will be time for the cake, then the party bags, and then the kids' parents will take them home and it will be all over and I will have got through it; and what's more, when I look at their faces and think of them chasing round after me and chasing round after one another in the maze, I know it will have been a success. When I catch up with that thought, I feel ecstatic, overwhelming relief; a burst of euphoria rushes around me like an injection of morphine, a sickly-sweet rush that makes me want to laugh and cry at the same time.

❦

After the kids have gone, the witch from Norwich comes down to the house to get her money for the afternoon.

"I hope you didn't mind my stepping in?" I say, still slightly out of breath and a little embarrassed at my previous bug-eyed ferocity. "I just felt the kids needed a bit of oomph!"

"Oh, that's fine," she says with complete seriousness. "The thing is, my act is quite subtle."

I give her the fee – I am too weary to argue – and she makes to leave, then stops, and turns back,

"By the way," she says, "will you be rebooking me?"

"To be honest," I reply, "no."

"Great!" she says blithely, not having taken in a word. Then she leaves.

I watch as the Vauxhall Corsa reverses out and is passed by a large Range Rover, driven by a returning parent who had already texted me a few minutes earlier about some items left behind at the party: a pullover, a missing Nintendo, a pair of trainers and a coat, all left by her six-year-old son. She is in a hurry, turning the car around immediately then winding down the window with the engine still running.

"Great party," she says as I pass the forgotten items in through her window. "That garden of yours is really special."

"Vikki wanted it to be something for days like today," I reply.

As I watch the car disappear down the drive, the wind just lifts a little and the leaves rush and shiver, a wave that rolls in and out, peaks, fades, then builds again.

It almost sounds like applause.

THE APPRENTICE GARDENER

1970s–1980s

When I was a teenager, in the late '70s, we lived at the end of a terrace of modern houses in Haywards Heath in Sussex. It wasn't a perfect location, as we lived next to the headquarters of American Express, a large gloomy brown office block from which their employees could watch your every move as you wandered around your house and sat in your garden. There was also a large local substation situated next to the front that made a buzzing sound as if someone were being continuously fried, which in hindsight was probably us. But there were advantages, too. As we were at the end of the terrace, we'd been given a narrow extra parcel of land, which meant that the garden wrapped itself around the house on three sides and was pleasingly spacious, especially at the back, unlike those belonging to the neighbours, pinched and narrow by comparison.

At the front of our house was a small lawn with beds on the edges that led down to the front door. In that bed were hydrangeas and roses and hollyhocks and the beginning of a flagstone path that led round the side of the house. At the side, next to the path, was a bare sandy area where we grew sunflowers up against the brickwork.

At the back of the house, the path finished up at the dining-room door, which looked out onto a patio dotted with bay trees in tubs, and beyond them the centrepiece of the garden, a square lawn dominated by a vast, unwieldy weeping willow on one side and a round wooden summer-house on the other. This was supposed to be somewhere you could sit and gaze out from, but quickly filled up with so much bric-a-brac – garden furniture, suitcases, cricket equipment, an unused gerbil cage – that it was difficult to even close the doors.

There were two further beds at the far end of this lawn and, if you walked between them, the garden sloped down quite noticeably to a high brick wall that marked the end of the whole plot. This section beyond the main lawn was awkward because of the slope and was never properly tamed; it was at various times a composting area, a wilderness and an attempted rockery. Another weeping willow on the left-hand side spread its branches over a large part of this bottom section, which was a blessing, as it helped to disguise some of the failings of the area around it.

All down the side of the garden bordering the American Express compound was a beech hedge; there was another beech hedge dividing our garden from that of our neighbours on the other side.

This garden was entirely my dad's creation. There had been nothing there when we had moved in, just bare ground with a hint of lawn at the back. He'd built it with his own hands and, in many ways, it reflected his own personality.

My dad liked to garden, but he liked to garden in a certain way. And he liked to garden in a certain way because he liked a certain kind of garden.

He didn't like neat, sensible, inoffensive gardens, the kind you see outside a million homes in the UK being tended on a Sunday by people in their sixties wearing slacks and sensible gloves and kneeling on cushions, the kind with neat lawns with precise edges and little fussy beds full of little fussy flowers round the outside and occasional little fussy water features and even a garden gnome or two.

If my dad ever saw one of these gardens, he'd screw up his face, rub his fingers together and make a mocking, high-pitched sound which sounded like "Winnywinnywinny", as if the people who made such gardens were lightweights, possibly even homosexual. Not that my dad was really homophobic – just capable of the odd expression of homophobia, the kind that was seen as inoffensive and entirely acceptable in the 1970s.

My dad hated small, neat, sensible gardens. He liked dramatic gardens full of big things. Big trees, big plants. Big, muscular, dramatic, noisy gardens that made an impact. He liked the gardens that you had to sweat over, that you had to hack away at with a mighty two-fisted implement rather than daintily nip away at with a trowel. My dad looked down on the trowel. I don't remember him ever using one; I remember him using his shovel and a fork quite a bit, but never a trowel. I think he thought that trowels were a bit "Winnywinnywinny".

My dad thought effort was the key. Putting your back in and sweating were important when you gardened. It said something about you as a person. He liked gardens that had this muscular, worked-on quality, hence the thick bushy hedges round the outside of ours, the towering weeping willows, the gigantic sunflowers round the side of the house and the hearty shrubs wherever possible.

It drew attention to itself, and when you walked down the road parallel to the side of the house (remember, we were on the end of the terrace), you noticed it. The hedge seemed to be spilling over into the American Express car park below it. The large weeping willows looked like nuclear mushroom clouds.

For all that my dad did like gardening and devoted some time to it, he still regarded it as a lesser art. He gardened, but he wasn't as passionate about it as he was about poetry, music, writing and art. Those were the deities. Those were what life was really for. Gardening wasn't one of those, though it still had to be done. It was some way behind in the roll call of great things to do – the Jewson Fixit League rather than the Premier League.

Nonetheless, he continued to pummel away at it for most of my teenage years, and in time he got us to pummel away at it too.

As we got into our teens, my brother and I were expected to help; it was our duty, apparently. We were paid for doing certain jobs, but it was pitiful pay – even by the standards of the 1970s. If you hacked at the nettles that covered the bottom end of the garden in blistering heat, you got 30p. If you picked up the unsightly high stalks that used to pepper the back lawn, you got 30p. If you worked all day – and I can only remember boiling hot days in the 1970s – you might get enough over the course of a week for a time-limited visit to the sweet kiosk at Haywards Heath railway station.

I didn't want to be doing that, and it wasn't just the poor wages. I had my own world to attend to. A world dominated by my obsessions – known as 'Thinks'.

Thinks weren't passing fancies or just interests; they were a whole way of life – obsessions that consumed me from the moment I woke up to the moment I went to sleep. They defined what I was, what I did, what I thought, how I dressed, how I spoke, how I behaved, my whole being. Thinks could be about almost anything: real people, sports, the arts, other countries and cultures.

Thinks could go on for years. Sometimes they overlapped. Sometimes it was possible to have Thinks that carried on behind other Thinks, then re-emerged when the first ones had been left behind, rather like a fire that lies dormant then suddenly flares up.

The complete list of Thinks in order, from my earliest years, ran as follows:

Dressing up as historical characters

Football

Playing the drums/jazz music

The work of Thomas Hardy

Apart from the dressing up as historical characters, all the other Thinks are still in play today. There was certainly no room for gardening, which felt from the outset like an awful imposition and a complete waste of time when I'd much rather be doing something else.

It wasn't helped by a lack of appreciation for the natural world in my family. We never watched nature programmes on TV. On holiday, we went to places where there were castles and museums and galleries, rather than waterfalls and forests teeming with wildlife. We didn't have a caravan.

We never went camping. We always went for a walk on a Sunday, but it was called a 'house criticism walk'. We'd simply wander around the town along various residential streets, pointing at different houses and saying things like, "I don't like the way that roof slopes", or "Those bricks are awful!" My parents never took us on nature rambles or pointed out foxgloves or lavender; they never talked about the miracle of how house martins flew all the way back from Africa with unerring accuracy to the tiny nests they'd built in the crook of our roof; they never talked about the life cycles of insects, or the rhythms of the seasons, or enthused about how, in summer, the sunflowers growing on the side of the house would bloom like a yellow-headed basketball team.

Mum wasn't an enthusiastic gardener any more than Dad was. Her domain was the house and the maintenance thereof – it was a very traditional 1970s marital setup. Occasionally, I would see her kneeling in the flowerbeds, gently pulling out some weeds with her yellow marigolds and putting them into piles (in this, as everything else, she was precise to a surgical degree), but that was rare. The garden was simply left to my dad.

I was never likely to have a gardening gene, and so it proved. I don't dislike gardens entirely, but if I like them at all, it is from a determinedly non-gardening point of view. I can appreciate them from afar if they are big, dramatic and well-kept (the big ones, not the fiddly-piddly ones – ah, the son of the father). I can look at them and enjoy them to a certain degree, the way I would an expressionist painting or a piece of sculpture, but I don't want to touch or feel or understand them. I don't want to get to know how they work or get under their skin. I want to look at them occasionally – not very often – take a quick breath of satisfaction, as I would do after swallowing a good ice cream, and walk away.

The first place I lived in when I graduated was Peckham – that is 1980s bombed-out, scabby, violent Peckham, not the coffee shop and artisanal bakery, trendiest-place-in-Europe Peckham of today. The house we lived in had a tiny square of garden that I didn't even notice.

It is probably just as well that I didn't notice it, because it was barely a garden at all, a patch of grass dominated by two burned mattresses that had just been dumped there, one on top of the other, at some point before we'd moved in, like a statement by a Young British Artist.

In the four years I was there, I never went in that front garden. Never touched it. Never thought, at least, of removing the burned mattresses. It was there, but it wasn't there – an unremarkable little tableau of decay that melted so seamlessly into the general landscape of barbed wire, broken fenceposts, paint-peeled, graffitied walls and grubby, curtained windows it might have been created by a landscape gardener. It seemed pointless and somehow even foolish to contemplate trying to change anything in a garden that fitted its surroundings so well. As if it might disturb the equilibrium of the place. At the very least it would probably have got us burgled more regularly.

It was partly also just my time of life. Truth be told, I just didn't see the mattresses. Even though they were directly outside my bedroom window, I didn't notice my surroundings at all. I didn't even consider I had a garden any more than I considered whether I had a countersigned will. I was in my early 20s, with that peculiar gift of selective sight that is given to the young that sees what it wants to and erases the rest. I wanted to be out conquering the world, getting drunk, not cultivating roses.

Later, in the early '90s, when I married Vikki and we lived in Greenwich, we had a 30-foot garden. There was a concrete sitting area that jutted out from the left-hand side of the garden where you opened the back door, covering two thirds of the distance to the back wall. There was a long wooden table on this with a primitive arbour that framed it, consisting of narrow wooden struts hammered together and covered with a token weave of foliage. To the right, on the other half of the garden, there was a bed of plants containing some poppies, a few grasses and a rhododendron bush – all of which never seemed either to flower and prosper or perish completely; they maintained a kind of steady mediocrity, achieving the distinction of just 'being', year after year, in a state of semi-drowsiness, the stems wilting but not totally brown, the flowers bent over in an attitude of dazed, somewhat weary repose as after a heavy night's drinking. But I was happy with that. At least there was something there that passed for a garden – something that didn't thrill but didn't totally let itself down; something which crucially always carried with it the promise of something better.

That was all I needed or had time for. It meant I could focus on sitting out at the long table that dominated the space and enjoy supper in a surrounding that just about held its own and yet, at the same time, let me wistfully dream about its future. It was a garden for the lazy, and at the same time a garden for the romantic. In effect, a garden for the non-gardener; my kind of garden.

Fast forward a decade and here I am, having swapped that for three acres – hedges, beds, shrubs, plants, a sunken valley, a beech maze, a firepit and nine lawns, and I only know the names of three types of trees. How did that occur?

Well, it seemed like a good idea at the time. More accurately, it was the idea of two battered, half-crazed, exhausted people, desperate for some joy. Years of Vikki's cancer treatment had seemed to empty our lives of the kind of simple everyday happiness that most people take as a right. When we saw the garden for the first time, it was like a door opening onto another world, a world that was not unfamiliar but from the distant past; a world of thrills, laughter and engagement. When we looked at the acres of green, we saw parties, magical evenings; we saw

a dreamlike space for playing music; we saw reading, pic-
nicking, yoga, charades, sleeping under the stars; we saw
herbs, food, interactions with nature. We saw a whole new
life of possibilities.

We didn't stop to think that someone had to deal with
the practicalities. The fact that everything grows. That
the maze, unless trimmed with monotonous regularity,
becomes an impassable thicket. That the Leylandii at the
side of the house grow so fast they can get a third as big
again every five years. That the beautiful, manicured valley
with its tropical plants and high banks, within a couple of
weeks each summer, quickly turns into the set of a Vietnam
war movie unless it is tended to from morning to dusk.

We were naïve, but then we were swept along at that time by a different energy, the one that doesn't care too much for gnarly detail or gentle reflection. It is the energy that wants to grab and snatch and plunder and not look back; that doesn't know if life is going to even be there tomorrow. When the vendor mentioned on one of our numerous visits that one of the beds had membranes to stop weeds growing, instead of asking what the other twenty had, we just nodded in a kind of satisfied way and accepted our good fortune.

Of course, I could have made myself a proper gardener; I still could. Make it one of my Thinks; throw myself into a period of intense study like I have done at other moments of my life and learn about garden implements and soil irrigation and how to nurture chrysanthemums, just as I have learned about the development of the catenaccio tendency in Italian football in the late sixties and how drummer Kenny Clarke's freeing up of his right-foot technique at Minton's Playhouse in New York in the mid-1940s changed the face of bebop drumming.

I have the right obsessive temperament for it, and I know people do get obsessed with it in that intense, quasi-religious fashion. I am good at immersing myself in a world, and there is no bigger, better, more encompassing world than gardening. Books, festivals, TV shows, lots of specialist gear. Its own language. Plenty of fellow travellers – everyone has a garden, and you can do it at all ages.

I could study, learn and improve. And I have moments where I can almost taste the possibilities. Indeed, I have started reading up about the subject, getting out books, rattling through pages online. There is a wealth of great gardening and nature writing, from Richard Mabey and Emma Marris to Helen Macdonald and Jenny Uglow. Already I've found some fascinating gardening-related stories. Roderick Floud in his wonderful book, *An Economic History of the English Garden,* describes how vast armies of young gardeners in the 19th century worked on the great country estates and lived extraordinary lives in bothies, tiny cramped cottages, not just sharing bare, cold, leaking rooms but beds, too; barely subsisting, working six days a week from dawn till dusk with only a slice of bread and jam and a cup of tea for dinner, whilst still being expected to go off and better themselves by wandering through the acres of garden studying the plant life. One gardener records in his diary his aim to learn the names of fifty plants a night!

Dedication, graft, asceticism – I can understand that; I can relate to it. More than once I have found myself day-dreaming about the possibility of becoming a gardening obsessive just like those men in their bothies (though I am not good with sharing accommodation and tend to get very hungry in the evenings). I can imagine complete-ly giving myself over to the gardening life, transforming The Valley into a tropical paradise with a lake at one end full of lilies and a brook that runs through its heart, the whole thing teeming with lush jungle-type plant life. I can picture the paradise I create – homemade sculptures with a strong South Sea Island influence in among soft grasses and delicate orchids on the steep banks; trees laden with rich fruits – kiwis, pomegranates, mangoes – the whole thing alive with the shriek of interesting bird species, stunning animals, and visible from viewing platforms on all three sides (my gardening fantasies always tend to the spectacular). I can imagine myself researching all the different plants long into the night and then applying this new knowledge from the moment the sun rises, and it is dramatic and exciting and there are deadlines and failures and setbacks as sculptures collapse and the brook blows its banks and trees crash to the ground in tornado-like gusts of wind, but I struggle on and on, working right through the night, eventually achieving a gorgeous, award-winning garden and some kind of spiritual awakening as a result, with the garden becoming a mecca for others, the basis of an Oscar-winning film and perhaps even an inspiration to recently diagnosed cancer patients (I said my gardening fantasies tend to the spectacular).

What makes this even more of a tantalising prospect is that, for perhaps the one and only time in my life, I know I have the most extraordinary raw materials with which to make it happen, this incredible gift of a space with colossal dimensions and wonderful natural resources: its rich soils, lush lawns, thick hedges and towering trees. Enough leaves to mulch down and fertilise dozens of new beds. Enough wood dropping down each year to build a bridge and a summerhouse, and still power the open fires of the house throughout a chilly winter.

There is just one problem.

I hate gardening. I think it's a stupid idea.

You make something beautiful in a garden and nature ruins it. Not once, not twice, but repeatedly. You clear away weeds or mow a lawn or put in plants, and then you must do it again. And again. And again. It's like writing a book and having someone just rip it up afterwards. Or completing a picture and having it slashed to ribbons with a kitchen knife. It seems frustratingly, existentially pointless.

And if I find no joy in the basic notion of gardening, I find even less reward in the actual processes it demands. It's not in my experience a thrilling interaction between you and the natural world; it is a dour, repetitive series of mucky jobs – hours and hours grubbing around on your hands and knees being bitten and stung, having passing birds shit on you, kneeling in rabbit poo and trying to pull weeds out with your bare hands because your gardening gloves are manky and the thumbs have holes in them. It's mindlessly hoeing soil and picking out endless bits, yanking deadheads off plants that disintegrate in your hands and cutting thorny chunks out of shrubs that either scratch you, cut you, or give you a pronounced skin condition, all the while knowing you are going to have to do this tortuous task all over again a week later while getting sunburned, bad knees, backache and covered with ticks.

People also say that when they are gardening, it's so relaxing they just think of nothing.

Just think of nothing?

How? How do you think about nothing other than what a totally pointless activity you are involved in and how you want to kill yourself? How do you do that? How can you be immersed in a spiritual nirvana when you are trying to get out the mangled hedgehog that is caught up in the blades of your ride-on lawnmower? How is that zen-like? How does that take you to a higher plane? How does it not just make you want to get a shotgun and put it in your mouth?

On the contrary, I have found gardening positively bad for my mental health. When I garden, my brain festers and frets and turns in on itself like an outsized, jellified ingrowing toenail. It wanders horribly, restlessly, seeking out ancient rivalries and fighting old battles. While I have been pruning rhododendrons or mowing grass or hacking away at patches of nettles, I haven't found myself spiritually remade and floating on a cloud of mindful bliss. I have, among other morbid reflections, revisited at least a couple of fractured teenage love affairs, tortuously retrodden a failed business opportunity in the 1990s, rerun a couple of bitter disputes with my family and even found myself seething with rage at the fact that my best friend in primary school said he was going to take me to the World Cup in 1974, then backed out three months before, claiming that his uncle had "hurt his head". What kind of a fucking excuse is that!!??

So here I am, the world's most reluctant gardener, stuck with a massive garden, an attitude problem and no way out. The warm weather has arrived and everything is growing, especially the thingy with the big, tall thingy that hangs down. What's more, we have opened for bookings over Easter, which is only weeks away and the clock is ticking. I just have to turn this garden around.

THE PILGRIMAGE

September 2007

I pluck two hydrangeas from the bank next to the seated area behind the kitchen; two that are still in relatively rude health.

I don't really know anything about hydrangeas, just as I don't know anything about any flowers, so I do some quick research.

Hydrangeas originally came from Japan, although were introduced to this country from North America in the 18ᵗʰ century. They can symbolise a range of emotions – the pink ones, gratitude, the blue ones, heartlessness and frigidity – but since the two outside the kitchen that are in the best condition are pink and blue, I decide to ignore this and just take both anyway; how they look is the most important criterion, and these are profoundly beautiful, perfectly shaped and dazzlingly coloured. The stem of the hydrangea can also apparently be used to make medicine for urinary tract infections and prostate problems, and the plant contains small amounts of cyanide; I decide to ignore that information as well, partly because I have already touched all parts of the flower and it is probably too late for me to do anything about this, other than make a mental note to go easy on the research next time.

Your eye couldn't fail to miss this bank of hydrangeas at the back of the house when they are in full bloom – they form an absolute riot of colour that you look on through the kitchen window when you are doing the washing up. Different colours bloom at different times. Those I have selected, the pink and the blue, are two of the later ones; the others have faded and turned a limp brown colour so that they almost seem to melt back into the bank behind them, propelling the blue and pink ones forwards, as if someone were holding them out towards you.

These two seem to be very perky; there isn't even the first hint of browning, and none of the petals are showing signs of fraying at the edges. When hydrangea flowers are finished, they are like old paper to touch, paper that just crumbles between your fingers, but these are still firm and resolute. When I brush my fingers against the edges of the petals, they give to my touch then jauntily flick back into shape.

It is ironic, really. These two hydrangeas are pretty much the only colourful thing in the garden. The rest of the three acres is just masses of greenery. I am grateful for them now in a way that I don't think I have ever been grateful, as they are just what I need. While some climb mountains in the wake of a loved one's death, or do charity bike rides, or turn daredevil and do bungee jumps out of planes, I am going to see The Police in concert in Amsterdam. I am taking the hydrangeas with me to lay on Vikki's seat.

I remember her buying the tickets the year before she died, with her laptop out in the living room, cursing and thumping the keyboard from time to time as she attempted to make the purchase. She chuntered and grimaced and then, after what seemed like hours, she wheeled away from the laptop and punched the air with a triumphant "Yesssss!" as if she'd scored the winner at Wembley. The whole exercise was a feat of endurance, conviction and bloody-mindedness. It was very her.

How could I not still go?

I feel I must travel alone. A lot of people might have considered asking a friend along, but the thought never entered my mind. A friend, I feel, might almost get in the way of the experience of grieving, of in some way being close to her.

I have a very romantic view of it all, though it also just feels like an obligation, a necessity. I am going to walk the streets we loved (we'd been to Amsterdam many times before), go to the restaurant we adored and, most important of all, lay flowers on the empty seat next to me at the concert.

I don't know why this seems so important – there have already been many floral tributes and there will be many more to come – but this journey feels special. Maybe there is something about the specifics of it: Vikki fighting hard to get these tickets, symbolic of her determination and desire to enjoy life to the full; my doing this trip alone now, signalling my own defiant ambition to go on with life even without her; even something about seeing The Police themselves, a soundtrack to our mid-80s courtship, the musical expression of so much of what we shared. It all adds up to much more than the sum of its parts.

The Pilgrimage

It's not just a visit to a Dutch football stadium to place some hydrangeas wrapped in foil on a plastic seat; it's more of a pilgrimage to a special place to make a lasting memory.

It must be these flowers, too, the flowers brought from home, from the garden she loved, not some flowers just picked up from a shop or the airport or a street vendor. It must be these flowers that we looked out on together and got excited about, in the garden she never lived long enough to enjoy (even if one of the flowers represents frigidity – she would have laughed at that).

Inside my suitcase, I have arranged my clothes in two piles on either side, creating a well down the middle. I have put the hydrangeas inside an oversized sandwich box and surrounded them with the gentlest of tissue paper before sealing them in and putting the box in the well. I don't know how long they will last in there, but they only have to make it through to the following night.

When I get to the airport, I have a last-minute worry as I check the case – one of those irrational panics I seem to be getting at the moment where I suddenly fear that there is some-thing horribly, awfully wrong; more specifically, that I have made a terrible mistake. Apparently, this is not uncommon in the recently bereaved; it's a manifestation of the shock of the whole experience, when your sense of security and wellbeing is suddenly attacked – a form of PTSD. Whenever this happens to me, random thoughts seem to spiral rapidly out of control, fear piling in on fear in a furious torrent, the worry becoming more ludicrous and overblown by the second. I am unable to stop it once it's started and I just have to wait for it to blow itself out, like a wildfire.

Do I have to tell someone about the flowers? I don't know why I would, but do I have to? Do I have to declare them in some way? Am I supposed to pay some sort of tax on them? Should I fill out a form? Am I importing horticultural products without realising it? Is it like the USA, where you can't even take in a tomato sandwich without being pounced on by sniffer dogs? (To be fair, this had happened to me five years before at San Francisco airport.)

Even worse, will they think they are something else, these flowers? Something illicit. Something banned. And then I panic, thinking of the drug offshoots – the prostate drugs, the cyanide. I am going to the Netherlands where they know all about drugs. It's the home of drugs. What are they going to think? Will I be able to explain my way out of it? Will they not believe me? Will I get a lawyer? Will I be able to contact one, even? I am not good with my phone at the best of times. Will they strip-search me anyway?

By this point, my suitcase has disappeared behind the curtains and it is too late, so I have the whole flight to churn and worry. Thankfully, though, since I am flying from Norwich to Amsterdam, it only takes forty minutes before I have landed and am reunited with my case, and I exit the airport without a problem.

The hotel I am staying in is further out from the centre than I thought, situated behind a noisy café. My room is depressing, with a musty brown carpet (I can hear Vikki tutting in the background, "You have to do the research!"), but it doesn't seem to matter.

I carefully unpack the hydrangeas, which seem unperturbed by the journey, fill a teapot with water, then sit them carefully in it. It looks oddly bonkers, as they are disproportionately huge, sitting there in the tiny teapot, and I am suddenly worried that they will fall over. So I slide the teapot next to the desk wall and prop the heads against it to take some of the strain. I then place two high boxes of tissues that I get from different parts of the room on either side of them, so the heads are almost resting on them, in case a freak gust of air should blow them sideways. Apart from writing down my mobile number and leaving it next to them in case of emergencies, there seems little more I can do to look after them, so I head out.

I walk and walk, along the canals, up to the north by the open harbour into the fierce wind. I walk back down southwards, past the picturesque, tall merchants' houses with their long windows and distinct gables casting haunting dark shadows. I walk through deserted cobbled squares, along tourist-filled streets, through tree-lined avenues where barges drift along the water more slowly than I am walking. I go as far as the fields south of the central canal ring.

You cover more ground when you are alone.

The walks remind me of Vikki and the things we did together, and that actually isn't as painful as I expected. It is more wistful on my part and curiously less emotional. Places still have a life of their own, an energy quite separate from your memories. They are as noisy and lively as they always were. They do not mourn. It is just you. I am carried along by the vitality of everything around me. I even find myself chuckling in some places. When I walk along a familiar canal where we'd been on New Year's Eve a decade before, I remember how someone set off some Chinese firecrackers literally under our feet, scaring the bejesus out of us. As I come to a familiar, quite innocent-looking street, I recall a woman who stuck her head out of a doorway and suddenly asked us both, "Do you want big humpy time?"

On that first evening, I go to our favourite Indonesian restaurant, but because I haven't booked it in advance, they can only let me have a tiny table squeezed up next to the bar, with a door nearby that keeps opening and shutting. I smile as the door flaps for the millionth time; this would also never have happened on Vikki's watch. The food tastes good, as gorgeous as I remembered it. It's just I don't have anyone to tell that to.

When I get back to the hotel, it is dark outside, and I open my bedroom door gently. I don't want to create a huge breeze and blow my flowers over. As I see that they are fine, I get another of those momentary glimpses when I realise my paranoia is absurd, but as usual it doesn't really change anything. Within a few seconds, I find that it has reasserted itself and I am looking at them in minute detail for any sign of decay, holding them up by the window. They look good. I sleep heavily that night.

The next day it's the concert and I set off for the venue early, in the late afternoon. I have wrapped the stems of the hydrangeas in some foil that I have brought with me and put them in a plastic bag that I hold. When I get near and start to wander through the crowds of people outside, I find myself carrying the bag not at my side, where it could get bashed about by a passer-by, but almost in front of me. As I continue, I hold it closer, tight to my chest, cradling it. It doesn't feel as if I am nursing some flowers, it feels as if I am protecting something far more precious – the very person the flowers are remembering.

When I get inside the Amsterdam Arena, it is heaving with people, the walkways outside crowded with concessions selling hotdogs and tour T-shirts, the most popular by far the beer stands, where people are buying enormous trays laden with pints and carrying them into the stadium.

There is an awkward moment during the bag search outside when the security guy looks inside mine and sees two hydrangeas.

"Flowers?" he says.

"It's a special occasion," I say.

He grins.

"For the band," he says, making a throwing gesture.

"No, they are for my seat."

He looks confused, but lets me in.

Inside, I find our two places and sit across them at an angle, which is useful because at regular intervals fans get up and walk past to purchase yet more enormous trays of beer to carry in.

When the music starts, the band on stage are barely visible, tiny stick figures topped with blond hair on a vast platform at the other end of the arena. When their faces suddenly loom large on the screens at either side, they are massive, disproportionate, brightly lit and otherworldly. The bass drum is a hefty thump to the chest that seems to reach you a half-beat later than the rest of the music and there is an eerie, almost ghostly quality to the performance.

They run through the hits, and I and thousands of others sing along. It is strange not to have Vikki singing next to me; not to hear her wonderfully eccentric, rebellious voice, no respecter of key or rhythm.

"What are you singing?" I would always ask.

"That's 'Message in a Bottle'," she would reply.

"That doesn't sound right."

"It sounds right in my head," she'd say.

All the while, the heavy drinking group of locals near me continue to go in and out, carrying more vast trays of drinks as the band plays on, each song a snapshot of a past life. 'Every Little Thing' was our first Greenwich flat, the sun streaming through the windows one Sunday as we danced round the tiny living room. 'Roxanne' I remember blaring out of a shop in Leeds once when we were visiting her parents. 'Don't Stand So Close to Me' we listened to whilst flopped on the sofa, exhausted new parents with our miracle, post-chemo daughter in the early 2000s.

Back in the arena, the end is approaching. 'Every Breath You Take' starts, probably Vikki's favourite Police tune of all. Some people are already heading for the exits.

At the end of that song, I make ready to leave.

The moment is here.

I carefully lift the hydrangeas out of my plastic bag, the one that I haven't let go of throughout the concert. I take a last look at them and see the edges of both are starting to brown and crinkle, but they are still defiantly colourful and I am struck by what amazingly durable flowers they are: flying here in a plane, surviving in a stuffy hotel room and walked through bustling crowds. I take them out gently, place them on the top of the upturned seat of the one next to me, leaning them against the back. It is a narrow ledge, and it takes a few attempts, but I manage to balance them there eventually.

For the first time, the thought strikes me: Why am I doing this? For what? A moment? A moment that will pass so quickly? The flowers look horribly precarious just draped across the top of the seat. Very soon they will, in all probability, be gone. Blown off. Knocked off. Picked up and disposed of by the army of cleaners who will sweep them up along with the many sweet wrappers and plastic beer cups and other detritus. Lost forever.

Yet, at the same time, I sense how I am absolutely driven to have this moment, however short it might be. This one symbolic gesture. It feels like some sort of victory, I can't explain why. It's a strange triumph but a triumph, nonetheless.

Having placed the flowers on the seat, I get to my feet slowly and I walk away. I try not to look back because I know that the moment has been achieved, and I want to keep that perfect memory in my mind; the place Vikki would have sat, the flowers there, a perfect reminder of her. Who she was. The flowers that grew in her garden. The garden that she loved.

Yet I do look back – progress is slow as we file out along the row, and in telling myself not to turn around, of course, it becomes impossible. I can't help myself. I am greedy. I have had the moment, but it isn't enough. I somehow want more. I want to imagine the impossible, that my flowers will stay there forever telling their story. That people will see them, and they will mourn, too. I want the whole world to mourn with me. I want the whole world to mourn Vikki.

So I look back, but as soon I do, I see the queue of people behind me moving slowly forwards and I see that one of them must have already brushed against the chair, because the flowers aren't lying on the back of the seat anymore. They are lying on the floor.

I am devastated. I want to go back and pick them up, but I can't; there is a queue of people following me. I want to wave and signal and ask someone to just rescue them on my behalf, but that is impossible above the din of the Tannoy. I want to tell the guy behind me and ask him to pass the message on down the line like a kind of Chinese whisper, but I can't think how I would explain it.

I wish I hadn't looked back. I wish I had just walked on. Then I would have kept that picture in my mind; the flowers draped on the back of the seat, the end of my pilgrimage, the completed picture, the last dab of the brush. As it is, I feel as if the moment has been spoiled. As if the pilgrimage remains unfinished. As if it has all come to nothing.

Maybe it is something in my expression, maybe just chance, but at that very moment, the fattest, loudest guy in the whole queue, possibly in the whole stadium, who is now standing right next to where I was sitting, for some unknown reason, stops and, mid-conversation, bends down, picks up the hydrangeas and, as if he somehow just knows, delicately lays them back on top of the seat.

THE PATH

February 2019

I am sweating, on my hands and knees.

It's three days into my proper, garden-saving schedule, and I'm trying to clear the main path that runs up from the road past the side of the house to the top section of my garden, a path about 40 metres long, which was once clear gravel but is now crisscrossed with thick patches of moss and grass.

My job is to lever it up, clump by clump, shake the gravel loose and dump the rest into my wheelbarrow before carting it off. You might think this a painfully labour-intensive method, but it is a last resort. A couple of previous attempts years before, where I paid people to come in and spray the area with weedkiller, just didn't work. They only succeeded in changing the colour of the moss rather than killing it off.

I am alone in this task, scrabbling around on my knees on the garden path; Emma has her hands full with the inside of the house. She has ordered new linen and zip-and-link beds for the rooms; she has done some sensational online deals for new cutlery, a dinner set, a dining table, extra chairs and a new sofa for the living room; she has even been able to source a free and virtually new, full-size table-tennis table for the room in the house that she wants to turn into a games room. She has also started fixing longstanding problems – a loose roof tile here and there, a redundant power point in the kitchen and a problem with the water pressure. She has a vast list of jobs on her phone that never gets any shorter. Deliveries arrive constantly at the new house. Her mobile burbles into life at all hours, like a child with ADHD.

Emma glides effortlessly through all this. Her parents owned North Norfolk's most celebrated country hotel, and it shows. The world of hospitality is deep in her bones. She has all the right knowledge and instincts. She is immensely practical and good with detail. She knows how to look after people's needs; how to charm them and woo them; how the customer is always right even when they are wrong. She is good in a crisis, at keeping calm when everyone around her is losing their cool. She is made for this.

I, on the other hand, am spectacularly not. I can switch on the ride-on lawnmower and guide it around the garden, but that is about it. I can perform very simple gardening tasks, but I have no innate knowledge. I have no instincts, no feel for what I should be doing. I can use a shovel, a fork and a hoe, but I don't know what to shovel or fork or hoe. I don't understand the gardening seasons. I don't know when something is alive or dead unless it is so dead that I can smell it from the driveway. I am hopeless with most kinds of machine or gadget (it took three demonstrations and a phone call to show me how to use the ride-on mower). Have I said I know the names of exactly three trees?

Essentially, I am a beginner with no tutor. A novice with no means of getting better other than experience, which translates into repeated failure I don't have time for.

The one thing I do have is a sense of urgency. It is the end of February, and we are potentially just weeks away from our first booking. This isn't just some frivolous deadline either, some sort of amusing, last-minute scramble where we shout and scream and collapse in a heap afterwards, laughing. This is serious. I absolutely must make this project work. We have a sizeable mortgage

on the new house and recently my TV writing career, which has provided my income for the last 30 years, has completely dried up. I am now 56, which means my fortunes in that industry are unlikely to improve any time soon, and even if I manage to get some work in a related field – teaching or tutoring in some capacity – that is unlikely to be enough.

So I must rescue the garden now, just as Emma needs to make the house work – it is a question of simple economic necessity, of pounds and pence. A successful rented property means that we can keep our new roof over our heads, and an impressive garden is one of the keys to that success. What's more, this garden, with its size and scope, could be an extra asset, providing the x-factor that might make the whole enterprise stand out.

There is another sense, too, why it feels really important to make this happen, and happen well. I want to make it work for Emma's sake. We've waited a long time to move in together and I don't want this special moment to be compromised. Moving to our new house marked a new beginning, a fresh start, a new and important phase in our relationship. Such moves are always exciting and life-enhancing, but they can also have their challenges. It's not all glamour when you are with someone 24 hours a day; it's dirty socks and bad breath in the morning; it's crabby moods as well as party smiles at night; it's all the uncomfortable, messy and poor moments, as well as the lovely, pristine, beautifully planned gestures. And given that there are going to be plenty of new issues to deal with as we take this next step in our lives, I don't want us to be handicapped by money woes too.

So, my taking over the garden is something very pragmatic. It's about the nuts and bolts of our being able to live together. It's about survival; it's about stability; it's about the most basic requirement – somewhere to live.

But then, it is also about something even more fundamental than that.

It is about *us*.

※

There were so many jobs to do in the garden, I could have started in a hundred different ways, but I reasoned that the main path that visitors would see on their way up to the house, and which they would walk along while getting to other parts of the garden, was as good a place to start as any.

So far, there have been three days of work with my brand-new trowel, down on my knees on an old cushion, jabbing and shoving just underneath the surface and prising up the clumps of moss, then picking them up in my mismatched gloves (I've just bought a new pair, but have already lost the left-hand one), shaking them free of any attendant stones, dumping them in a wheelbarrow and inching forwards, or rather inching forwards and then sideways – the path is wide enough to drive a car down.

It is curious how little has changed about the design of basic garden implements. According to *Country Life*, October 11th, 2007:

"Metal-shod wooden spades were used in China from about 1,600 BC, and the Romans were the first to use metal spades in Europe. The pala, which was recognisably a spade with a broad blade, was recorded by Pliny as being the ideal tool for opening up rushy ground. Hoes are even older. 'Elementary hoes with a triangular flaked-stone head, mounted on a handle with thongs fixed with bitumen, are known from the fifth millennium BC in Mesopotamia,' wrote Anthony Huxley in his charming *Illustrated History of Gardening* (1978). Later, angled hoes occur in pre-dynastic Egypt; and very much later, settlers in the New World observed that a large clam shell attached to a pole created the perfect hoe, as William Wood observed in *New England's Prospect* (1634)."

There has obviously been some fine-tuning. Spear and Jackson have, in the last few years, launched a new spade with a stirrup on the back, which means you can apply pressure more evenly rather than having the spade go wonky because you've pushed on either side of the shaft with your foot. They have also fiddled with the angle of the shaft, so it corresponds more accurately with the angle of the blade as it enters the soil. In essence, though, I am working with the same gear as a bunch of people who've been dead for more than a thousand years.

Apart from the weedkilling sprays that I have already discarded as an option, I have looked at a couple of other modern possibilities, including a contraption that can be fixed to the ground that then lifts the surface, rather like a gardening can-opener. While ensuring that the path is lifted to the same extent each time and is therefore less haphazard than the freehand trowelling, it strikes me as not much quicker and even more tedious than the method I am currently employing, since you have to keep setting and resetting the screws. There is something about the simplicity of just swinging a blade that I prefer. It is highly physical and tiring, but then I would rather be tired at the end of it all; I would rather feel exercised – that my effort has resulted in some sweat rather than just some mental frustration. At least I can take that away from what is a tedious, repetitive slog.

I try not to look up ahead and see how much I still have to go, but I can't help it. Neither can I resist making these ludicrous contracts with myself – if I can just get to the bit where the trellis is falling down, I'll have a break. If I can just get to the bit where the hedge has grown over the side of the path… If I can just… If I can just…

The trouble is, I keep falling short of my goals, and instead of inspiring me, my targets just become a source of frustration; a new accusing voice shouting at me in my head.

"You can't even get to the trellis, you lightweight!"

"You've only got to the bit where the hedge grows over, you wimp!"

"Christ almighty, a ninety-year-old would have cleared the path already and had time for a sit-down and a cup of tea!!!!"

⁂

It doesn't feel like a good start. And I had hoped for a good start, despite my previously held prejudices about gardening. I had hoped for something to happen once I started. *Something.* A feeling whereby the work became more than the work. Where I discovered that elusive thing Victorian poets wrote about, that special peace, that spiritual connection with nature. Where I suddenly discovered it anew and found what thousands, millions of other gardeners have found before me – that huge sustaining bond. Me on my knees in nature. Next to nature. In nature. Of nature. Becoming part of nature and being transformed by it, remade and invigorated by it.

Just a bit more than an overweight bloke in his fifties hacking at a driveway with his trowel.

I have started reading Richard Mabey, the great nature writer, for inspiration. Even though his background is a million miles from mine – he grew up wandering through the Chiltern Hills near the family home and has spent the whole of his life since then cataloguing, studying and writing about the natural world and man's relationship to it – I can still admire the strength of his passion. When he writes, in his amazing book *Nature Cure*, "And then in late May, after all the false starts and unfulfilled days, summer opened, as if it had been waiting for the right moment. And not just any old summer but what was to become a season of burnished colour and intoxicating smells that banished elegies for days 'like they used to be' and burnt itself into Eastern England's collective memory..." I haven't a clue what he is talking about, but his sheer, blood-summoning commitment just seeps off the page. His descriptions are a testimony to the strength of the bonds he feels.

But for me there is none of this connectivity. I don't see burnished colours or intoxicating smells or spirits. I just see the metallic edge of the trowel edge hitting the path and hear my own laboured breathing. My knees hurt immediately, even though I am on a cushion.

In one sense, I can see that it was naïve and faintly ludicrous to expect much from this first day's work, and especially from just trowelling a path. Even I understand that the rewards of hacking at gravel in light drizzle in February can't be expected to deliver in spiritual terms in the same way as, say, the moment when glorious summer is revealed in all its brilliant splendour, but it still doesn't stop me being a tad disappointed.

I am impatient – always searching, reaching. I am always looking for things to be more than they are. Just gardening doesn't seem enough, somehow. I couldn't just start weeding a path. I have to be setting out on a full-blown spiritual quest. But it isn't like that. At least not right now. It is absolutely what it is and no more – hard, dirty, physical labour.

So I just keep my head down – literally. I arrive in the morning at the place where I was the night before with my head bowed (you can see a clear line in the stones between the bit I've done and the start of the next batch of green moss). Then I sink to my knees and start hacking away again. I don't look up. I just look down at the little patch in front of me. I shrink my world. I try to concentrate on every detail of what I am doing – a kind of Buddhist approach to trowelling. I have no thoughts, other than trowelling. I AM THE TROWEL. The trowel is me. All I think of is trowelling. *My Life as a Trowel. To trowel or not to trowel. Oh, What a Lovely Trowel. The 39 Trowels.*

I concentrate on becoming totally immersed. I want the path to become moss-free. Having set that standard at the beginning, I have to continue with it. I can't let anything go. I can't suddenly just leave a bit. "No one will notice" isn't an option. *I* will notice.

Slowly I advance, and when I have finished for the day, I get up and back down the path a couple of steps, still with my head bowed like an obsequious courtier leaving the presence of the king, before turning and heading to-wards the car.

My knee blows up and my legs are stiff, but I keep trowelling. My second finger swells up at the joint, but I keep trowelling; there is a red mark in my hand where the back of the handle has left an imprint from gouging the drive.

Days merge into one another. I forget the hours, the minutes, the seconds. They are all the same, punctuated by the same rhythms, me kneeling on the cushion, taking the trowel back, then thrusting it forwards just underneath the surface. Lifting the moss, shaking the stones off and depositing it in the wheelbarrow. I have become very good at it now, and consistent. I no longer have those moments, as I did earlier on, when I occasionally crashed the blade into the ground too deep, so it didn't want to go in, and the jarring sensation went right up my arm to the shoulder. Equally, I no longer misjudge the depth the other way and go in too shallow, so it scuffs off the top and I shoot forwards as if catching a crab while rowing and end up spreadeagled on the path.

Now I can do it with my eyes shut – and I do. I think of trowelling the path. I dream of trowelling the path. One evening in the middle of my trowelling odyssey, we are watching TV and Emma asks me, "What are you doing?" And I look down and realise that, as we are absorbed in a complex police procedural, my right hand is making an involuntary gouging motion.

Once, just once, when I am in the middle of trowelling the path one day, I do that thing I told myself never to do. I do that thing that I swore would be suicide. I look up and immediately realise what a huge mistake that was, for I see that I have about twenty metres of the path still to go.

The disappointment is massive. The sense of failure huge.

Will I ever finish?

I get a trowelling depression. I feel like a failure because I haven't made more progress. I thought I was further on. Much further on. I am a wretched human being. I have not accomplished what I should have. I am a slacker. I'm not very good. And my mind goes. My trowelling technique goes. I start making wild swings with the trowel to get up bigger and bigger chunks of moss over a wider area. I forget about what I have learned, about distributing my body weight properly, about having the trowel blade at a certain angle and not taking it too far back before thrusting forwards. I just start whirling the trowel around loosely.

I start to feel pointless for engaging in this, for trying to turn back the tide. Suddenly I see the path as a metaphor for my whole gardening ambition. I stand up and suddenly realise – this a full-blown horticultural crisis.

There is only one thing to do; I must get my head back down again and trowel my way out of the slump. *Must.* Nothing is going to happen unless I do it.

So I kneel straight back down and I start trowelling. I start trowelling when all the voices in my head are saying, "Stop trowelling, you idiot, stop trowelling!" Then, one day as I'm trowelling – *I am the trowel, the trowel is me, The Sound of Trowelling, Guys and Trowels, To Kill a Mocking*

Trowel – I dare to look up and I am nearly at the end. I am about a metre away!

It feels like a miracle. Like the trowelling gods have smiled down upon me. I redouble my effort and I trowel twice as fast, and the clumps are flying up in the air and I am hurling them so fast in the direction of the wheelbarrow that some of them are missing but I DON'T CARE. And my technique has gone to the dogs, and I am swinging like a madman and hacking and even turning the trowel over and jabbing down with it as if I am stabbing someone.

I am seized with a manic intensity. I just want to get to the end, and I can see the finishing line, the very end of the drive just creeping into the upper edge of my line of vision. I HAVE WON. I HAVE WON. I stand in triumph and feel mighty, fulfilled. As powerful as Zeus. Zeus trowelling.

As I go back to my car, I look up and see the hedges that are uneven, the beds that are still thick with weeds, the patchy lawns, the roses that are straining to beat off nettles as they struggle to climb trellising. The whole garden a creeping, gloomy presence reaching out in all directions like an invading army.

I am overrun and need help. Even if we can't afford much of it, surely we can get someone to troubleshoot, pop in for a bit, give some advice, calm my fraying nerves. Supervise. Point. Save us.

When I get back, Emma is beaming from ear to ear. We have our first booking for the Easter weekend.

The Path

We celebrate, and then we realise... It is only five weeks away.

ATTACK OF THE KILLER ONIONS

September 2007

It is five months on from Vikki's death.

I am a little steadier, a little more stable. I am establishing a new life, a new routine.

My bereavement still wears at me and some days it can overwhelm, but as the months have passed, I have learned that I can survive with it, and that, crucially, it will be part of my world forever. I have started to get used to this new existence that carries with it some of the old and it's starting to feel manageable; that it still has good things in it and isn't just something ghastly that was foisted on me by circumstance.

Having to take care of a young daughter by myself has proved the biggest reward, as well as the biggest challenge, and a welcome distraction too. Romy is six, at an age where I have to feed her, help her dress, brush her hair, take her to school, pick her up again, then take her to her friends for playdates and parties, and to her dance classes and riding lessons. Just being absorbed in her life has helped me avoid too much introversion, and I am healthily preoccupied with her needs, mentally taxed and pleasantly exhausted at the end of each day.

I also have to organise the house – keep it clean and tidy and functioning and turn my mind to improving some of the interior. The bathrooms are dreary and tatty; the kitchen is an ancient, country-pine confection of cupboards that won't shut, indelibly marked surfaces and creaking, unreliable applianc-es. And there is my work too, as a TV writer, which has lain dormant but which I must return to now and reinvigorate. This means time and application and inspiration.

The garden is, not surprisingly, the lowest of my priorities. I whizz round the lawns on my ride-on lawnmower when I can, then race back inside again. I try not to look too hard at the rest of it.

That flutter of excitement when Vikki and I first saw it, that sense of wonder at its amazing scope and size, has largely disappeared. I can still get a thrill when I open the curtains of my bedroom and see the sun dancing on the tops of the trees, or when I walk into The Valley and feel staggered by the lush banks on either side that seem to rise and grow around me as I descend into its lowest point. But now, often, the garden seems a rather ponderous reminder of my situation: how I have little time to devote to it now I am a widowed parent; how many of those dreams Vikki and I shared for what it could provide must be postponed or else forgotten altogether.

Moss has grown through the membranes of the path. Bindweed has spread out like a giant spider's web across the large beds at the front and back of the house. Patches of nettles have sprouted in every conceivable space, clumps of pointed, spiteful annoyance like teenagers hanging about in provincial towns; you get rid of them in one place and they spring up in another, leering at you, refusing to go away. The paths through the maze are growing over. Tree branches are hanging above the drive and even scraping against the front windows. The lawns have bare patches and little ridged circles of earth like models of Iceni hillforts, where I have scattered molehills with my boot.

I am still, nearly three years on from when we first arrived, discovering new things about the garden, which makes an interesting change from just worrying about the old ones. Previously hidden items from decades ago pop up in the former quarry that is The Valley all the time. As if summoned from their burial mounds by some mysterious ghost, they just appear from time to time in the top of the soil to catch the eye or a stray ankle: an Olivetti typewriter with half the keys missing, a wooden children's chair, a length of Scalextric track, the broken tip of a Dymo gun, the lid from a game of Kerplunk – a veritable museum of the 1970s.

While hunting for a missing tennis ball that has been walloped from the play area at the top of the tennis court into The Valley, I also find the crumbling steps of another abandoned path, completely hidden under a mulberry bush that has grown over, and even stumble on a new, bamboo-laden, grass-stuffed little hideaway, like a priest hole, tucked away behind a thick avenue of beech hedge in the maze.

Then there are the onions.

Attack Of The Killer Onions

I have known about the raised beds on the front lawn since we moved in, but typically have never investigated them properly. One day, trying to calculate if they are worth keeping (I have decided to try to simplify the garden if I can before it overruns me completely), I find myself looking at them more closely, picking at the earth rather carefully and ineffectively in the manner of someone who knows nothing about plants. The stems above ground give me no clue as to what might be beneath, so I eventually lose patience and just yank some out. I find to my surprise they are attached to clumps of bulbous and healthy-looking brown onions. I pull and pull, clearing the front part of the bed, and build a mountain of onions next to me that should be worthy of some sort of government subsidy.

I remember an early conversation I had with Vikki about self-sufficiency as we looked at the huge garden before we bought it and imagined what we could do – what it could give us, how it could transform our lives. I get very excited and suddenly see the advantage of this unexpected treasure trove and, without knowing what I can do with them, I project forward, not practically, as a normal person would, with the notion of maybe storing the onions then cooking with them, some soup, perhaps, some sort of pickling, but to the other end of the scale, with the speed of a bullet from a hunting rifle, envisaging some sort of mass production, onion-something and a lot of it; the whole garden transformed into a giant nursery – if I can get this much out of one bed without even trying, Christ, I could feed Africa – my own brand of onion products, success, a whole new career, a new way of life, selling them locally at the end of the road then to markets and shops; forming a company, expanding, then selling off to an American conglomerate before leaving the countryside altogether and buying a fuck-off apartment in London with a window box, something which, as I have started to struggle with the contrasting demands of a six-year-old daughter and this enormous house and garden, has come to represent all my dreams of escape rolled into one.

There are certainly enough of them. The beds seem to burrow down to the very core of the earth. There isn't just one layer of onions; there are several. And when I think I have reached the basement, there is another beneath that.

I bring them into the house and wrap them up in newspaper, piling them in the kitchen under the butcher's block in wicker baskets, where we normally store the saucepans, and they are in bowls and vases, and they are in biscuit tins, in old cardboard boxes, even in old shoes I no longer wear.

And as I do so, I dream away about my onion future and feel a real rush of excitement. This is a project. This is an opportunity. This is exciting.

It is clear to me later, when I look back at these events, that I'm not entirely in control of my thoughts and feelings at this point. I am very much in that post-bereavement phase that is really only the next stage of bereavement, where you are out of the immediate fog but just as vulnerable and imbalanced, in a different way; where you snatch at things like a child would sweets; where you are impulsive, irrational and your mind is an unsteady, volatile creature, prey to all sorts of new ideas, flash enthusiasms and dangerous passions.

You want to be carried away as fast as possible from what has just happened, from the pain and emptiness, the despair and the shock of losing your loved one. You want to move things

on; you want to speed up time. And one of the best ways to do this, you feel, is to throw off your old life and undergo a personal makeover – whether that means becoming a bungee-jumping, cliff-diving daredevil, a sculptor in Berlin, or indeed the onion king of East Anglia. It is a seductive thought, that all you need do is assume a different guise and you can somehow cast off the chains of the past, even though, as you quickly realise, it is a misleading one, too. Bereavement is the passport you must take with you, whatever the new destination.

So, I become obsessed with onions. I dig up more and more, and no sooner has the kitchen filled up than I put some in the utility room and under the stairs, and I keep on digging, because, although I still have no idea what to do with them, that somehow makes me dig up more, thinking I have to have enough to cover every possibility.

The more I dig, the more onions appear. It seems as if there is a secret conveyer belt full of onions and operated by elves, who are shoving them up into the holes so that, as fast as I empty them, they fill up again.

Soon, there are onions all over the house – I even have a bag beside my bed – and it is possible to detect a lingering smell everywhere, a woody, aromatic hum that hangs in the air. It adds to my sense of anticipation – it feels as if there is a vital new presence in the house, a new guest. I may be no further on knowing what to do with them than I was at the beginning, but they are here under my roof and it is surely just a question of time. I have another satisfaction too, especially on a day when the rain beats down on the roof or the winds lash at the door, that the harvest has been brought in and a natural cycle completed. I have been a good farmer. I have looked after my crop.

For a couple of weeks, this sense of wellbeing continues. I am quite proud of what I have done, and I tell friends and show them when they come round. When they ask me what I am going to do with the onions, I boldly declare that all options are on the table, because they are, and it is easy to talk in possibilities, and I take pride in the sheer size of my crop, even though I still haven't the foggiest idea what to do with it next.

Gradually, the onions start to get in the way. Because I have had to empty so many receptacles to store them, the contents of those receptacles – the saucepans, plates, dishcloths, books, photographs, clothes, board games – are now in different places and I have trouble locating them, which interrupts my routines for cooking, cleaning and looking after Romy. Every time I try to find something, I find onions. There seem to be more of them all the time. As if they are breeding. Or maybe just moving around to annoy me. It doesn't take long for the sight of onions to turn from an exciting one full of potential to an irritating reminder that I still haven't found a solution.

I start resenting the onions – the imposition on me, the changes they have wrought, the way I have been invaded. I don't think about the fact that I invited them in. I start to get cross with their presence. In reality, of course, I am annoyed with myself, though I can't admit it. It's obvious that the ambitious, industrial-scale manufacture of onion-something was just bullshit, but I still haven't got any other sort of plan at all, other than making a lot of onion soup. But how much onion soup can you make? And how the hell do you make onion soup to start with?

In the end, I give up. I shut down. I ignore the onions. I pretend that they aren't there. I blank out the woody, bulbous smell. I look at the baskets of newspaper and just think of them as baskets of paper, not the keys to a new life. Instead, I focus on Romy and my own sanity – on the next day and the next.

Time passes – it is hard to know how long. The days and weeks still flash by, yet seem an interminable drudge. One day I unwrap one of the balls of newspaper and find the onion inside has gone sticky, with print now visible on its outer skin. I unwrap a few and find more and more of them have gone off, the outer skins green and tacky. Some are even more decayed, quite black, and furry with fungus like cotton wool. The worst are just mush, a viscous slurry pasted across the paper, no longer even recognisable as onions.

I panic. I unwrap more and more. They are nearly all rotten and I can smell something new – a sickly, cloying odour rather than the hearty, optimistic, woody hum from before. I unwrap them all, faster and faster, more and more dismayed, until there is a pile of paper in the corner of each room and the smell has become an overwhelming, ugly stench. I am left with a mountain of oozing carcasses all collapsing into one another.

It is too late – the whole crop has been ruined. It's over. I have no alternative but to get rid of them all. I collect the wheelbarrow from the garage and fill it up with these sad, tatty remnants, wheel the barrow down to the bin at the bottom of the drive and throw them all in.

I feel overwhelmed and depressed that I have let this happen – and on this scale. Not one or two onions, but an entire harvest spoilt. It feels callous and somehow sickening. I feel nausea, less to do with rotten, smelly onions and more a sense that I have done something very wrong.

Once again, I fear I have not lived up to Vikki. I have failed her and her plans. I have let her down. Failed to realise our dreams. I haven't been quick enough, smart enough, sensitive enough.

But I have failed nature too. I have wasted its resources, refused its help, and that feels bad in a different way. Through *my ignorance and lack of sensitivity, I have eschewed its gifts; gifts that could have helped myself and my daughter; gifts that were God-given and natural. Gifts that have been wantonly spurned.*

I feel more estranged than ever from nature now, from any understanding of it, from bonding with it. I know less than ever where I am with myself and this garden. I can't ignore it – it feels like a legacy I must honour – but I just don't know how to make it work.

A voice in my head says that this is all further proof of the madness of the whole project; that I should walk away as soon as possible; that it's extravagant and a waste for an overworked widower and his only daughter to be surrounded by this vast Eden; that I should pass it on to someone who can do it justice and unlock its rich potential.

Yet still I can't let go of the thought that our future is at this place – a future that Vikki fought so hard for, that we all fought so hard for. Still, I want to find a way for it to work for us. To find a way for us to work for it.

So, I go back and forth in gloom and frustration, unable to see a way to make things better, unable to stop looking for a solution. It's as if we are all – myself, my bereavement and the garden – perfectly trapped, chained together like prisoners, thrashing around in a frenzy, trying to unravel our shackles, all the while getting more and more entangled.

MARTIN

February 2019

I need help. The moss-strewn path has taught me I can't do it alone.

When I look online, most of the local websites that advertise gardening services look like they have been built by a three-year-old and usually have one image – a picture of the gardener standing in front of a small, barren flowerbed with brick sides that looks like a model of the exercise yard at HM Prison Belmarsh. They generally have awful graphics, someone's mobile number that you can never get through to and a landline that is always answered by the gardener's bewildered wife, who says she will pass on the message and never seems to. Then there's always one review, probably from the gardener's mother, who says that the person in question "couldn't have been nicer".

I've had gardening help in the past, but it has always been via word of mouth. The first was Bobby, a friendly local man. He was reliable and strong, and doggedly hoed and trimmed and mowed on the two half-days that I could afford him, but it was never more than a holding operation – and a failing one at that.

When he arrived, it was a question of which three or so jobs he should undertake out of the thousand that needed doing most that day. When we had decided which three, he trudged off, returning to the house a couple of hours later, red-faced and exhausted, to collect his money, only to announce that, as usual, the list of jobs was over-optimistic, and he hadn't even completed the first.

When Bobby finally departed – he became a carer because there was a regular pay cheque, but I suspect he was also a little depressed by the pointlessness of his gardening role at my house – I ended up employing a company rather than an individual.

For some reason, I thought this would improve things greatly, but because I could only afford to pay them for the same amount of time as Bobby, relatively little changed. The garden continued to get worse and fell into further and further decline, becoming tatty and more decrepit, like a street sleeper after a couple of years outside. The only advantage with the new gardeners was that, because they were a company, they could call on greater numbers when required and could, when my finances allowed, do the odd big blitz in which they would bus in a whole load of people to temporarily rescue a particular section of the garden from total oblivion.

They were a good, solid outfit, but I never felt they formed a real bond with the garden, mainly because they weren't there often enough. But they did well for several years, at least slowing down the decline, chipping away at the mundane jobs like mowing or pruning before suddenly pouncing on a piece of overgrown greenery just before it keeled over and died.

They did these blitzes but also special projects. They put in new steps on the paths into The Valley and handrails to go with them.

They created new fencing when the old trellising around the tennis court collapsed. Importantly, they were good at manufacturing cheap solutions, at re-using old materials and making do.

Another issue I had to deal with was pest control, as moles were one of the biggest problems I endured, and still do. There are open fields on two sides of my house that run up to the edge of my garden, and there are nine lawns in my garden, each of which provides the moles with a holiday home when the fields nearby are tilled and they are looking for a break.

Hugh was the mole man, a quietly spoken, urbane and charming individual somewhere in his 50s, who reminded me of one of those progressive rock band musicians from the 1970s; the one who left just before they became famous and made all the money, who possibly took too many tabs of acid, went a little weird and ended up being picked up, half-naked, by the police trying to thumb a lift back to his parents' house somewhere in Cambridgeshire.

He would turn up in the garden in true Norfolk fashion, often unannounced and grinning in an alarming serial-killer sort of way (which is, I suppose, what he was to the moles), placing what looked like a series of giant bulldog clips into the ground at selected points in the molehills, then leaving. When the moles walked into them, the clips would snap shut and the creatures would literally die from shock. It sounds gruesome but was quick and effective and preferable to gas pellets, which are hit and miss depending on the dampness in the soil, and sonic wave machines, which some moles apparently just embrace and think of as mole Muzak.

It was £25 per dead body, and when Hugh got one, he stuck it in a plastic bag and tied the bag to the front door to prove it: no corpse, no fee. He sometimes didn't let us know when there was a kill and so we were left to piece together the evidence that something had happened – a disappeared bulldog clip, the screech of his ageing Mini Metro as it left and a dead mole rattling against the knocker when we opened the front door.

When my rescue mission begins in earnest, the gardening company are still with me. Much like Bobby, they are still – with the limited resources I've supplied – fighting a valiant, but rather grim rearguard action, a kind of gardening Dunkirk. But now I definitely need something more. I need someone who can help me reverse this decline and change the whole picture.

Emma and I have agreed that we should put a little more finance into this and stretch to two or three days a week initially to get the garden up to standard, so now I just have to find this person, hence my searches online and my fruitless encounters with the local gardening community, the drab websites and the pictures of the exercise yard at Belmarsh.

Then I get lucky. One day, the gardening company come to the door with someone new in their ranks. He is in his late 30s, extremely friendly and seems to glow with a healthy, outdoor sheen. He also wears a neat, official-looking polo shirt that doesn't scream comput-er repair man.

When he starts his work – he has to hoe the front bed and shape some of the shrubs outside the front door – I sneak a look or two and notice how quickly and smoothly he does his work. He seems at one with what he is doing, totally engaged with his task, as if he knows he is in the right place and he wouldn't rather be doing anything else.

Emma and I are immediately excited, and when he comes to the door to tell us he has finished, we make a point of both being there.

It seems he has come up from London quite recently. The gardening company were just the first to give him work, though he is ultimately looking to establish himself on his own. He exudes enthusiasm, not just for gardening but my garden in particular.

We mention our plans and he is very keen, and within a short conversation it seems we have found ourselves a new gardener.

His name is Martin.

SHAMELESS

May 2008

Romy is on the trampoline, but I am only half looking at her and the two other children she is playing with.

I am paying rather more attention to the 30-something woman who is standing next to me. She is tall and dark, with gorgeous eyes and a soft, kind smile. She is self-possessed and calm. Very calm.

I've invited her round because it is her birthday and we have already celebrated in the living room with a cake and some food bought from the local deli.

I've invited her round because she is new to the area and I didn't think she should be on her own on such a special day.

I've invited her round because her daughter and my daughter are friends and sit next to each other at school.

But most of all, I've invited her round because I fancy her.

We met at her daughter's birthday party, to which Romy was invited a month ago, and chatted in the gardens outside, the event delayed because the entertainer she'd hired, an animal balloonist, was held up on the A148.

Emma had also suffered a huge loss – her husband died even younger than Vikki – and we immediately had much in common, but there was a genuine connection too. We commiserated about the life of the single parent, shared stories of eccentric teachers at school and laughed at the bizarre and awkward post-bereavement advice some people gave out – I was encouraged to take up hiking, while one woman suggested to Emma that she learn to play the harp.

When I got in my car after the party, I was both pessimistic and enthusiastic. A relationship with another bereaved person felt just too easy and predictable, so it made me suspicious, but at the same time it was irresistible, and I knew I was going to see her again.

It has been more than a year now since Vikki's death, and I feel ready to meet someone, even if that feeling is shrouded in apprehension and guilt as well as anticipation.

❧

"So, this whole bit of the garden was added about ten years ago – it used to be a caravan park."

I make a sweeping gesture with my right arm and Emma exhales, impressed. I am conscious of trying to make my voice sound nonchalant, but I am at the same time aware of the impact of saying that part of my garden used to be a park.

Any nerves have settled quicker than I thought they would. I feel buoyed up by my surroundings. The garden is providing the script. The conversation is all around me.

In fact, if anything, I have gone the other way. Now I am showing off and I know it and I can't stop myself. I can hear my words and my gestures, and they sound smooth and slick, and even then, I don't want them to end.

The garden is making sense for a change, this time as a kind of pickup line. It is showing off with me; it is strutting its stuff. And if that seems crass and crude, then I still feel entitled to the moment. I have had so much darkness and dourness recently, I feel I am owed a little Vegas.

The garden is lifting me to somewhere I haven't been before, at least not in a long while. I am feeling strong and empowered, and I have rarely felt that since Vikki died. Too often, I have felt small and unsure and reduced. This new feeling is fresh and welcome, and if it's a little bloated round the edges, I'm just too delighted at the novelty of it to look too closely at the detail.

I have already led Emma and her two children up from the house, past the swimming pool. We have then crossed the path and wandered down into The Valley, and they have been amazed by the steep sides and the towering eucalyptus trees and the giant Gunnera, and the way we just seem to have been swallowed up by the silence. They've wandered up into the maze and got lost in the hidden pockets of space lined with bamboo in the middle; they've come upon the firepit area and seen where we pitch our tents when we camp underneath the stars. Now all three children are on the trampoline in the play area.

I have already heard her children's delighted reactions – they are six and eight, at an age where their feedback is nothing if not truthful – and I have seen in her eyes and heard in her voice too a sense of the wonder you feel when you first encounter the garden, the sheer overwhelming plenty of it all.

I am filled with pride. I almost can't remember the last time this garden made me feel so happy. Hitherto it's often been a worry, a drain, a problem that has been teased over but never solved. Today it has been a pleasure.

I talk of my grand plans, of what I want to do, like a cross between Capability Brown and Walt Disney; how I would quite like to build a Japanese Karesansui garden outside the dining-room window; how I might throw a zip wire across The Valley and transform it into an adventure playground; how I am thinking of purchasing a traditional traveller's caravan and placing it in The Valley for Sunday supplement sleepovers; how I might get the local university first-year students to freely display their sculpture in the priest holes in the maze. How I could have treasure trails too, free jazz festivals in The Valley, yoga retreats and mindfulness conventions.

I know I am going too far, though I can't stop it; I hear my own shameless attempts to strike the right family-comes-before-everything-what-a-great-single-father-I-am-quite-possibly-marriage-material notes, saying with a nonchalant throwaway chuckle that I'm not going to win a Chelsea gold medal but hey it's just great fun that the kids can run free and that's the most important thing isn't it?

It's a pose and a pretence, but it feels liberating to escape my old self for a bit – the uptight worrier who has obsessed at least twice a day since Vikki, Romy and I first moved here about the fact that moss is growing over the path, the shrubs and hedges need pruning and that the oak tree near the dining-room window is so huge it looks like it's going to collapse in a gale on the roof and kill whomever is inside at the time.

I even quite like this new person I am hearing – they seem far more relaxed and much more ready to laugh. I'd like to hear from this person more. I am fed up with the hard-working worrier. I know who I would want a relationship with.

Emma looks round as I speak and I can tell she is impressed, and as the kids play, I am conscious of our proximity and the garden is there in the background, but in the foreground, too, like the third wheel, the other best friend in our relationship that has brought us together.

After, when we have returned to the house and eaten in the dining room, when she has gone, I feel like going outside and high-fiving the garden that has helped me, that has made me look good, that has lied on my behalf.

I don't feel in the least hollow or superficial, as perhaps I should. I just feel bloody great.

CHRIST-WITH-A-SPADE

February 2019

On the first day of work with Martin, I plan to get rid of an old wooden climbing frame. The frame has sat in a little dip next to the tennis court for nearly 20 years, since well before we moved in. It was originally immovable and sturdy, a series of hefty oak logs bored into one another to create an impressive three-sided construction with horizontal steps every couple of feet and vertical posts about a metre apart, like an enormous clothesline. At one end, there is a rope attached to a tyre to swing on and at the other, a large net, like the ones used to disembark troops in World War II newsreels.

Over the years, in the wind and the rain, the structure has weakened and the logs have acquired a thin, green, outer skin of moss. Some of the joints have loosened and a couple of them have fallen off. More alarmingly, if you lean against any part of the frame with minimal force, the entire construction rocks back and forth as one, lurching and buckling into strange shapes, like an elderly drunk. Emma and I have visions of visiting children sliding off and being buried under piles of collapsed timber, which isn't the kind of thing you want mentioned in your first review. So we've decided that it must go.

By the time I arrive on this first morning, about an hour later than I expected, Martin has already dismantled the frame and even chopped up the long, tubular lengths of oak into recyclable logs for the fires. He has removed the logs and stored them elsewhere, and the site is clear apart from a thin covering of loose bark chippings, originally put there, rather optimistically, to soften any falls; it is almost as if the climbing frame was never there.

As an opening statement of intent, it is impressive and a little intimidating. I am already nervous, as this will be our first day as partners and we will be working together now quite intensely for the next few weeks and months. I don't know what to expect. We are employing Martin, but he obviously knows a lot more than I do, so in terms of his experience, he is actually the one in charge. I am already nervous about this duality; how will that work?

I am also nervous about the fact that this is our first proper encounter. I don't want to muck it up and sound abrupt and embarrassing, which is my tendency when meeting people for the first time, especially when we are in an employer/employee relationship.

With the woman who comes in to clean the house, I have never got beyond the initial "What an awful day!"

Which is what I have been saying for years every time she comes to the door, generally following a quick glance up at the slate-grey Norfolk sky. The only alternative being, "What a lovely day!" on the rare occasions that the sky has a hint of blue.

Either way, after one of these two phrases, there is always a pause and then I say, "If you could just start in the kitchen..." and slink away.

That's it. It never changes. And I can never imagine it changing. That is how we communicate – the cleaner and me. It is set. We both know it. That is how we do things.

Of course, I am fully aware that she has different conversations with other people. It is not that I am wallowing in a sea of ignorance. I know there is another world out there. I have witnessed other people come in on day one and slide effortlessly into fully formed exchanges with my cleaner about her family and history and schooling and holidays and dreams for the future. My sister-in-law once came to stay and, after only having met her a few minutes earlier for the very first time, had the kind of emotional conversation that involved giving her a hankie to dab her eyes.

So it isn't as if I don't know the other possibilities out there – they are just not for me.

But I also want more from this relationship with Martin than a hurried greeting every morning involving the weather. I want to establish a genuine rapport. I am, perhaps foolishly, already thinking of Martin as a gardening guru.

I want to learn from him. I think he might be my bridge into the natural world, the key to understanding so much. He will be an accelerated learning programme. I might not have to bury my head in gardening books and websites for the next year if I can get to know him properly and pick his brains.

The climbing frame might have gone, but it has left a sizeable dip that now needs to be filled in with a layer of topsoil and reseeded. Once that is done, it will complete a playing surface that could host games of football, frisbee, outdoor skittles and the like.

Martin is going to level the surface. My job is to provide him with the soil to do it. Getting to this division of labour has already been painfully angst-ridden.

"So, Martin, how can I help?"

"Whatever you want to do…"

"What would you like me to do?"

"Whatever you're happiest doing…"

"I'm happy to do anything…"

"Great. Whatever you want to do…"

A beat.

"I was thinking, er…"

"Yes, sounds GREAT!" he says. "If I do the… er… er…"

"I KNOW. Why don't you level the ground?"

"You sure?"

"Yes, fine. PERFECT. PERFECT."

"Then maybe… er… you… er…"

"I KNOW. Shall I bring the soil to you?"

"Is that okay?"

"OF COURSE. PERFECT. GREAT. FANTASTIC!"

"FANTASTIC. PERFECT!"

There are 47 trees in the garden – a mixture of oak, birch, eucalyptus and elm, or so Martin says. Apparently, the average tree has anything from sixty thousand leaves up to half a million in the case of a mature oak, so even at a conservative estimate that means something in the region of five million leaves have fallen on my garden since the onset of last autumn. Each year when they have come down, they are collected up over winter – this was the last big blitz job I gave the gardening firm – and dumped onto a gigantic leaf mountain in the patch of waste ground next to the play area with the trampoline. Over the years, the millions of leaves have piled up and rotted down, compacting and solidifying to form a long and very solid plinth about 30 feet long and 3 feet wide, which looks like a scale-model of one of those rocky outcrops you see in the background of old Westerns. It's an obvious source of soil, a short wheelbarrow ride from where it's needed, and Martin leads me out from the play area to the leaf mound.

He carries his spade on his shoulder like a rifle and it doesn't break his stride, whereas I keep changing hands with mine because it feels awkward, and I end up nearly tripping over it.

When he gets there, he climbs on top of the leaf mound and brings his spade down very precisely a few inches from the front edge of it and, when it sinks in, levers it back and forth, shaving off a chunk of rich, brown, almost black soil that tumbles forwards effortlessly as if in slow motion. Martin then jumps off the top of the mound and chops the chunk up skilfully by sinking the spade in and turning over the soil, softening it, getting rid of lumps and grinding it down into a fine powdery flour. As he does so, he peers at the soil with all the relish of an addict chopping lines of cocaine.

"That's lovely stuff," he purrs.

He then gets back onto the mound and repeats the process. Clearly, he wants to make sure that the soil is the same quality further along the plinth, but I can see he also just loves doing this.

I watch him closely, the way his spade sinks into the leaf soil with a satisfying *thisth* sound. How he eases it back and forth. How he jumps down off the plinth when the soil is released and gets to work on it, chopping and thinning; the way the spade just seems to like being in his hand, and the way it expertly massages the earth. I swear I can almost hear the spade murmuring, "Thank you, Martin. Thank you for letting me be your spade," and then I could swear I can hear the earth murmuring, "Thank you for turning me over." And it is easy, just so easy – it is as if the spade is moulded to his hands, another limb, a part of him which has no weight, that takes no effort. As if it floats.

Then he stops, and it feels like the moment when the kung fu master has demonstrated and his younger apprentice needs to step in.

"Do you want to have a go?" asks Martin.

I can't say no, so I take my spade and climb onto the pile just the way he did it – or rather, I clamber up in a slightly more workaday version of his salmon leap, using the spade on the way up as a crutch.

Then I try to copy him, the way he uses the spade, the gentle persuasion of the blade, the smooth, loving action. I'm even conscious of trying to relax my body and look as happy and smiley as he does, even if every time the blade hits the cliff edge of the earth, it is as if the vibration goes through my body like a 50,000-volt shock and I want to shout, "FFFUUUCCCKKK!!"

I try, as well, after I have cut some earth away, to then slice it and turn it over several different ways like Martin does, but when I use the spade to do this, it is an altogether more brutal and desperate business – like someone killing an intruder. I employ a lot of force and the spade goes in a little too deep, as if it has stuck inside someone's skull. I have to wrench it out afterwards, and I stumble back slightly before pitching forwards to hit the bastard again just so he doesn't come up.

I try not to make too much noise, to betray the fact that it is all an almighty effort, but still, the satisfying *thisth* of the spade is overshadowed somewhat by the heavy grunting noise I make that sounds a bit like someone taking a dump in a wind tunnel. "WEEEARRRGGGHHH!!!!!"

There it is, or at least my version. A pile of soil, full of lumps and bits of gristle that weren't visible when Martin did it. A different colour, too – not that consistent rich, dark tone, but a patchwork of browns and blacks shot through in one corner with an inexplicable cloud of sickly green.

But Martin isn't put off. He doesn't seem to notice the difference, or if he does, he isn't saying. All he cares about is the dark, rich, fertile soil that continues to cascade down, albeit rather more reluctantly when I have released it.

"Look at that… Really good stuff," he purrs, his enthusiasm undimmed. If anything, by now, his voice has become even more reverent, more affectionate; softer and full of genuine tenderness.

Because he is in love. He is clearly in love with it, like other people love their wives or husbands or partners or children. He is in love with the soil.

How does he do that? How do you get to the point where you truly love soil?

How is it possible to look at decayed earth that probably contains the faeces of a million animals and actually relish it? At one point he sounds so enthusiastic, I could swear he is about to bend down and eat it.

I have no love for soil. I can't imagine ever loving soil. Thomas Hardy's description of harvest is lovely. Max Roach soloing on 'Salt Peanuts' with Dizzy Gillespie and

Charlie Parker is lovely. You can't equate these things with soil. Surely?

I start to wonder. Do I think anything not man-made is beautiful?

I can sort of see that a view is lovely, but in the way it is lovely on a postcard or in a photo. I like to frame it and put it in my own mind's gallery. I like to filter it through a human prism. I don't want to put my hands or feet in it. I don't want to smell it. This is essentially why I am fine with looking at pictures of animals and I just can't stand the real thing. The closer you get to nature, in my urban mind, at least, the uglier it is, the more it smells, the more it is likely to poo in your lap or bite your children.

But loving *soil*?

I know that for Martin, it's different.

Where I want to be distant from it, he can't get close enough to it. I want to step back from it. He wants to step in it. And not just step in it, but rub it all over himself.

In that moment, I realise how different we are. From what different worlds. Me – closed-off, suspicious, tentative, wanting to look at life from behind a screen with gloves on. Then there's Martin – open, smiley, touchy-feely, carefree and fearless, stretching his arms out to his natural surroundings.

In that moment too, I realise how far I am going to have to come to join Martin's world. It is his world, this natural world. I am an intruder. I am a stranger. Like an out-of-towner walking into a bar as the place falls silent and one of the rotten-toothed barflies spits viciously onto the floor.

I am going to have to go a long way if I am ever going to get close to it, but more than that, I am going to have to change a lot on the way. My views. My very senses. My understanding of what is beautiful. My notions of what I want to touch, embrace, get close to. I'm going to have to find a different perspective. A different set of instincts. I am going to have to find a different me.

It is a daunting challenge and I immediately wonder if I'm up to it. I'd like to try to close that gap, but is it just too far? Have I left it too late? Can you remake yourself and your relationship with nature after years of conditioning? Is the relationship with nature, as the word suggests, a natural thing? Is it impossible to renegotiate anyway?

For the rest of the morning, I fill up the wheelbarrow with my uneven, lumpy soil and wheel it through to Martin, who is waiting with the rake in the sunken rectangle next to the tennis court. I carry barrowfuls through and empty them into little hills on the top. Then he rakes the hills out… beautifully, rhythmically, the rake just kissing the surface of the soil and distributing the earth with evenness. He is so good at getting out the manky bits of old root and twig that I can't seem to weed out, and by the time I return with the next load, the hill I dropped previously has been dispersed immaculately, making the smooth carpet of soil a little more complete.

I notice fairly early that I am making a mess of the leaf plinth. Before, when Martin sunk his spade in to test the soil, he kept an immaculate line along the edge, but as I have gouged out successive loads it has become erratic and uneven. But then I have already given up on that. It only takes three or four trips with me prising the soil from the leaf plinth and carrying it through to start feeling fatigued, and whatever ambitions I had towards refinement are quickly abandoned. All I can think of is supplying Martin with soil, however messily.

I have to leave after a couple of hours, though I promise to return and continue later. When I do, the leaf plinth looks quite different from how I left it. The front edge of it is now neat and squared off; any remnants of soil that I hadn't picked up with my shovel from the ground have been removed and the area is clear, as if it has been swept.

Martin appears. "I just sort of tidied it up," he says, smiling and rather apologetic. "Hope that's okay?"

"Of course," I say.

It doesn't make me cross that he has tidied up after me; it makes me almost well up with sadness. I feel guilty I haven't done it better and I'm embarrassed. I feel I've let him down. I think again about the state of the leaf plinth I left and realise it must have looked like a bored seven-year-old had just spent the morning trying to destroy it by using it as a trampoline.

Martin smiles back, of course, and as he is near the soil again, he can't resist just gently dabbing at it with the end of his spade. He is far too nice to say, "You did a really shit job." I don't think it is in his generous, straight-forward character to play subtle mind games and try to undermine me. Of course, he might also be too mindful of our employer/employee relationship, but I think it is more than that, too, as if he somehow, quite genuinely, wants to help me. As if he wants to lead me gently by the hand towards a greater truth he knows. As if he indeed wants to be my guide. As if, in his own uniquely modest way, he has taken my sins on himself and made them his, and somehow atoned for them.

As if he is Christ-with-a-spade.

CHRISTMAS

December 2008

It is the Christmas after I meet Emma.

The garden is blasted and ugly – a shapeless mess. It had been improved in recent weeks by the addition of some snow, which had transformed the garden into a Disney paradise of fantastical shapes, with trees like magnificent temples and shrubs like graceful sculptures, but now the snow has almost melted, leaving white blotches on the surface of the ground or grim little puddles.

Christmas has long been our special family time, when we come together at our house in Norfolk. Vikki started it all when we first moved in – she embraced the festive season with a childlike enthusiasm. Both sets of parents, an aunt and Vikki's sister would come and stay, with fleeting appearances from my two brothers, and there would be a dazzling programme of events. First, the usual visit to the tiny, eccentric local church on Christmas morning, where we'd sing hymns to the keyboard accompaniment from a CD that kept getting stuck (Hark the h-h-h-h-h-herald angels si-si-si-si-sing). Back at home we'd have several rounds of the game Hedbanz, where a person has to put on a headband with a word on it they can't see, then guess what it is, aided by clues from the others. This led to some surreal moments, including the sight of my 80-year-old mother-in-law sitting with the word 'Brothel' on her forehead. Then, on Boxing Day, we would get in a fleet of cars and drive down to the coast to see the mad people of Cromer rush into the freezing cold sea and wince as the St John Ambulance tended the stricken on the beach afterwards.

Recently, there'd been innovations too, including our very own Strictly Come Dancing *competition, in which each couple had two days to learn two dances and perform them in front of a panel consisting of my mum and aunt. This new tradition had already assumed a cosy familiarity – I would dance with Romy and throw her over my shoulder and around my hips, endangering the light fittings, only to be tagged "showy" by the steely judges, while my dad, who always danced with Vikki's mum and moved slowly in a circle because of a disparity in height of nearly three feet and the presence of his catheter, was – more understandably, I thought – invariably held to be "lacking in adventure".*

The tour of our fabled garden was one of the longest established traditions of all, perhaps the oldest, as it had started the first Christmas we moved in. It hasn't really changed since then – a complete circle of our three acres, taking in the front garden then sweeping up along the straight main path with The Valley on the left and the swimming pool on the right, past the garage then up into the open grassed area with the tennis court, left into the maze, round, then into The Valley and back to the house once more. The Grand Tour – the complete experience.

My dad is older now and stays in the house, and Vikki's parents are less likely to come as well. Even if they do, the walk is much more limited – a slow wander up the main path to the play area at the top, a brief pause and then a gentle walk back down again, shuffling rather than striding.

My mum, however, never misses it. She has never got over the garden and how extraordinary it is. Coming as she does from a council estate in South London, and a thin, parched square of lawn the size of a gym mat in front of a tiny, terraced house with a shining front step – her mother scrubbed it every morning at dawn in an extraordinary act of ritualistic devotion – my garden has held for her an almost mystical allure, like the Hanging Gardens of Babylon.

Somehow, it seems to represent everything she has always believed in: working hard, bettering yourself and, above all, escape – escape from her stultifying upbringing, the limited aspiration, the defeatist acceptance of the status quo, the in-grained conservatism.

Where she'd come from, lives were laid out in strict order and dutifully followed to the letter: hard labour during the week for a pittance – the men lugging sacks of coal upstairs, cleaning trains, digging ditches, the women struggling to feed too many children, taking on extra sewing in the evening. A thankless grind for six days a week, the only respite Sunday (not for the women, of course, just the men) where the real treat was that you could get drunk most of the day and you didn't have to shave. That was it, that was all of it. You worked, cursed and fought, you drank to forget and, in the end, when it was all over, barely left a trace – a trinket or two, a lucky charm, a few threadbare clothes and the rent book on the dining-room table. That was life for many in working-class London in the '30s. A thankless, dreary cocktail of pessimism, fatalism and rage. They never expected anything better. They resented anyone who did.

Every so often, a brave soul would poke their head above the parapet – dare to dream of wanting more, wanting something else. Mum was not the first, though she might well have been the second. Her Uncle George before her had navigated such a path, found his own way to get out, not just escaping to a different land but rocketing to a different planet altogether.

Born blind, the youngest of nine, he had shown a phenomenal instinctive talent for playing the piano, starting in the local pub. Against the advice of his father, he left the pub and joined a showband on Park Lane. Within a few years, he was making wartime recordings for the BBC. Before the decade was out, he was living in New York and playing the hippest of modern jazz with Ella Fitzgerald.

He launched his own quintet, invented cool jazz and sold a million; he wrote 300 tunes, including the standard 'Lullaby of Birdland' that has been recorded by everyone from Peggy Lee to Amy Winehouse; he played for three American presidents at the White House; there is even a whole page devoted to him in Jack Kerouac's iconic On the Road.

He never looked back. He never really went back. He didn't even attend his parents' funerals back in the UK. Rather like my mum, he had nothing in common with the old South London world of booze, frustration and low expectation. Interestingly, he always stayed in touch with her, his niece, and we as a family would go to his concerts; she also went to see him in New York, and when later in life he came to the UK for the summers, not to South London but to a beautiful, bucolic retreat in the Cotswolds, they would always meet up. They enjoyed each other's company. They could talk about music and books and the things they loved. They could enjoy the new world they were both inhabiting while somehow still acknowledging their special bond – the background which they had both in their different ways escaped.

So, my garden for Mum symbolised that escape. It encapsu-lated it in a torrent of green, in the great sweeping valley and the lawns and the tennis court. It was a visual representation of her struggle to get away in its size and scope and gran-deur, in the way it was wild and indulgent and reckless and could be whatever you wanted it to be. In its sheer ambition. It showed her how far I had come and, by extension, how far she had come too.

You can see it in her face as she looks about her now, a smile falling on her like a gentle beam of light. She talks little; the words generally evaporate. She is too busy just looking, left and right, above and at her feet, stopping momentarily to take in the scene before letting out a little sigh as she sees something new. A little shake of the head follows, a disbelieving shake, as if she has witnessed a baffling magic trick or a great gymnastic feat, then she starts again up the path. There is something wondrous about the freshness of her response, unedited and spontaneous; she is like a young child unwrapping her Christmas presents.

It is me, my mum, my daughter, my sister-in-law and her mother in today's walking party – my daughter immediately racing ahead. The others, bar my mum and I, continue in pursuit of her as we lag behind; my mum seems to be going slower than usual. As we approach the tennis court at the top of the path, they are already heading back, and pass us in the opposite direction.

When we get to the top, I notice how tense I feel. My chest is tight and my breathing is thin and shallow. My mum stops ahead of me, turns and looks at me with a smile. A pleading, solicitous smile. A smile that is, in its own, gentle, disarming way, insistent as an armlock.

"Did you want to say something?" she says.

She knows I do.

She has always had a sixth sense about her boys, when there is something important unsaid, locked away. She just knows it. She can feel it. She doesn't even have to be in the same room. Many is the time I have felt her intuition from the other end of the phone – she once detected something wrong when I was in a different country.

When she knows there is something there, she is good at drawing it out – ever so gently, with a look, a soft squeeze of the hand. She is clever in many ways, the mildest of interrogators, but she is at the same time relentless, though it is never done because she is nosey or even merely inquisitive; she just worries when things are buried. All she wants to know is that everyone is okay, or that we are all right with the fact that they are not.

"What did you want to say?"

I do want to say something, though at this moment I just can't find the words. This information seems so enormous that I might as well be telling her that I have just murdered someone.

The truth is much simpler, though.

I just want to tell her I've met Emma.

❧

On the surface, it shouldn't be that difficult.

It is not that I haven't told anyone, I have – a few close friends, my brother, my sister-in-law. So it is not as if the information is new, being unfurled for the first time. It is also very unthreatening. I have met someone and we are just getting to know each other. I am not announcing an engagement or revealing that we've just got hitched in the Bahamas.

On the other hand, I am still emerging from the death of my wife, and it seems a huge statement to make, to declare that I am in any kind of relationship with another woman, that I have somehow moved forward beyond the events of the past. It's a complex and difficult thing to acknowledge. Especially when the person I am telling is my own mother.

So, it has been a logical thing to do... to pick my moment carefully... to broach the subject gently... to explain very carefully that, er... well, er... er... er... er...

Now the moment is upon me, and I am hesitating.

This is crazy. I am a 44-year-old man. She is my mum – a sympathetic, sensitive woman. We've always been able to talk, though she has respected my privacy and never pried. She has always been available.

Yet there is real apprehension.

❦

The relationship between mothers and their sons' girlfriends/ partners/wives is a tricky one – a constant, shifting, uneasy blend of dependence, intimacy, rivalry, fondness and suspicion, and I am only too aware of its potential hazards.

The relationship between Vikki and my mum was fine but could be distant. On the surface, they were quite different – Vikki was self-contained, while my mum responded better to open arms and the kind of female bonding and emotional intimacy that was not Vikki's forte. My mum wanted a daughter-in-law who would ring her up and share her innermost thoughts, but the road to Vikki's heart was firmly signposted with the words: "Need to know only."

There was frustration on my part that I could see both sides and felt that neither saw the other for what they were. My mother never quite recognised what an emotional, loving and warm person Vikki could be; Vikki didn't realise that my mum wasn't looking for an emotionally incontinent daughter-in-law, just an occasional sentimental gesture.

And somehow, in the middle of that emotional disconnect, I'd built up an anxiety about it all, too – that maybe there was a hidden problem, a great intractable difficulty that I hadn't recognised or addressed, rather than a simple difference of personality, which was probably what it was. That I hadn't seen it and thus had maybe even contributed to making it worse.

So I had yearned, deep down and for many years, to bring them closer, to literally drag them together – these two women, the two most important in my life until Romy came along, who seemed at times infuriatingly far apart. And the fact that I hadn't managed that had nagged at me, drained me and ultimately left me feeling disappointed.

That disappointment had left its mark – a wound that refused to heal. Little surprise then that now I was hesitating in telling my mum about Emma – suddenly it felt that wound was being pushed, poked and prodded; that there was unresolved soreness and pain.

❧

I want to tell Mum now. Right now. This minute. But I can't.

I want her to like Emma. I want it all to work. I want it to be fine.

But I worry it might not be. I worry about it being a repeat of the past, an imperfect relationship that exists in an awkward void of politeness and civility, that teeters above crisis, so it never blows apart and has to be put back again, an ancient grumbling steam engine that you wish would just collapse completely so you could rush out and buy a replacement. Break it up and start again.

And I plain just don't want to go there again – I can't. I just haven't the strength. In my post-bereavement world, I am depleted emotionally; I feel as if I have used up all my under-standing and intuition. I need things to be simple, clear-cut wherever possible, to fall into place without effort. Right now, I find it difficult to negotiate anything complex – especially the hazy swirl of human relationships.

So I am pulled in different directions; ready to speak but wishing to keep the whole thing under wraps. Willing and able to make the announcement, but worried about where doing so may lead.

"How is everything?"

"I, er…"

"Yes?"

I can't stall any longer.

"Good, yes… I've actually met, er…"

My voice trails off. The words get stuck in my throat.

❧

There is an image I have of my mum that I think really sums her up.

In the early 2000s, my dad had a bout of septicemia that almost killed him, but he recovered, thanks to his own indomitable spirit, some excellent medical care and the extraordinary devotion of my mum. Slowly, the colour had returned to his face and his wasted limbs had regained some of their sturdiness, until he was able to sit up in his hospital bed. On one of those days, I visited him and when I walked into the ward, I saw her by his side – she was combing his hair and doing it so gently and beautifully, and with so much love and tenderness that he looked for all the world like a cherub from an Italian fresco being tended to by an angel.

Family was everything to Mum. Everything.

She had lost hers at a young age: her mother died of cancer, horribly, at home when Mum was a teenager; her father drifted away from her in an alcoholic haze. She was alone and terrified.

She met my dad during that storm. They were good for each other in those dark days, and they were good for each other ever after – devoted, a true team. Her quiet efficiency and his theatrical messiness. Her calm solidity and his poetic flights of fancy. Her thrift, his extravagance. Whenever he made some crass pronouncement or angered a neighbour, she was there, working behind the scenes to patch things up like some skilful mediaeval courtier – a soothing word here, a quick telephone call there, that reassuring squeeze of the arm, the sympathetic rolling of the eyes from behind his sightline.

They shared lots, too – loved the stage and films and acting and music. They listened to the radio and went for walks together. They gave to charity and supported the local church. They watched Wimbledon every year. They laughed as one. They even wore matching hats and, later, had an unerring ability to forget names and details, which led to conversations worthy of Pinter.

"What was the name of that chap?"

"Erm…"

"You know… the tall one."

"Um…"

"He was in that film with that other chap."

"Alan Bates."

"No, taller."

Most of all, they agreed on family – its importance, the way it should be, how it should build a secure wall round you all and protect you, keep you warm and wanted, provide a solid base, help you spring into the air with a confident shout when it came time to make your own way in the world.

Above all, they both felt that family should always be there – when you need comfort, when you lose a partner.

When you get a new one.

❧

Back at the tennis court, a light drizzle is starting to fall. Soon it will be time to head back. There's no time like the present. I feel fuzzy, confused. Uncertain. Maybe I could do this another day. Another time. When it doesn't feel so much... like this. But then that's just putting it off, and I am here now. And looking at my mum, part of me feels I have already come too far. I have committed to this moment.

"I wanted to tell you something."

"I know you did."

She squeezes my hand.

"I've... er..."

"Yes?"

"I've..."

She nods. She knows there is more.

"I've met someone... And..."

"Yes?"

The nerves are biting now like an angry dog. The next bit rushes out of me. An uncontrolled torrent of words.

"Er... Obviously it's early days and obviously, er... we are going to see how it goes and obviously, you know, we must take it slowly..."

"What's she like?" she says, cutting through my defences.

"Well, she is... I don't know... Er..."

"You can tell me."

"She's, er... just a... a... a... lovely person... Kind."

Suddenly I hear my own words and they feel so inadequate. Weak. Trite. And I feel like someone else is saying them. Someone next to me. And I am sitting nearby, just wincing.

"And thoughtful… and caring."

Now I regret the whole thing. I've done it so badly. It has sounded woolly and feeble. "Kind, thoughtful, caring…" Emma's not a nun. I wasn't ready to do this. Maybe I will never be ready. I feel foolish. Stupid. Regretful.

"It's early days…" I say again. "I'm not sure…"

I feel myself backing down. Turning away. Embarrassed.

My mum squeezes my hand approvingly.

"What else matters?" she says, smiling.

THE CRAFTSMAN

I have started reading Thomas Hardy again.

He was one of my original 'Thinks' and I read him exhaustively for years when I was growing up. I studied the love poems for O-level, *Tess of the d'Urbervilles* for A-level, and wrote one of my least appalling essays at Oxford on the relationship between *The Mayor of Casterbridge* and the coming of the Industrial Revolution. In many ways, Hardy's words and thoughts gave voice to my teenage years.

I hadn't read anything of his for a while – several decades, in fact – and then recently, while out looking in a local bookshop for yet another gardening book to help supplement my meagre knowledge, I came across a new edition of the collected poems I didn't have and that rekindled my interest.

As soon as I picked it up, I realised what I had been missing.

There is something about the emotional intensity of his writing that clearly spoke to me all those years ago, the sense of hopes held, then dashed; unrequited love, thwarted ambition, bruised optimism. Such things appealed to the adolescent me, uncertain, confused, hopeful of finding his place in the world but often finding setbacks.

But if it chimed with a great deal of my teenage angst, it also now seemed to speak to my recent adult experience and all the shocks and disappointments of the last few years – the thwarted plans of a young couple, the abrupt and awful sense of loss, the challenges that follow in the wake of any death, regret, guilt, the onset of, at times, a paralysing pessimism.

There was something else, too, that suddenly seemed amazingly relevant – Hardy's view of nature; something I'd been aware of before, but distantly. Nature not just as atmosphere or background, but as a primal force, a whole personality, possibly the most vivid of all the characters he created – a living, breathing, joyful and sometimes terrifying presence that moves and shapes and colours the lives of those in its midst.

In *Tess of the d'Urbervilles* there's the erotic description of Tess secretly approaching Angel Clare in the garden "now damp and rank with juicy grass which sent up mists of pollen at a touch", the thrilling abandon of Beeny Cliff in the poem of the same name as the huge energy of his love for Emma finds expression in "the opal and the sapphire of that wandering western sea and the woman riding high above with bright hair flapping free", and the massive looming presence of the eternal Egdon Heath in *The Return of the Native,* where the travails of the characters are played out against a backdrop that eventually overwhelms them.

This is humankind and nature in a symbiotic relationship and, crucially, a highly emotional one. Flowers and fauna and trees and waterways not just as natural objects, but complex and profound gauges of the world, capable of giving joy and happiness and support and encouragement, as well as being hostile, indifferent and threatening.

Previously, I have always regarded nature as other, alien, different, and I have circled it suspiciously, backed away or jabbed at it with a stick like someone prodding a body to see if it reacts. Hardy's notion of nature brings everyone and everything together. It is inclusive. In his eyes, we are all part of the same circle. We are interdependent. Nature isn't always benevolent or an ally; sometimes it can be harsh and hostile. But it is, at least, our equal.

The more I read of Hardy's words, the more I can feel the possibility of a new tie, a resetting of the boundaries in my own relationship with nature. I start to see how it might be possible to get beyond my previous definitions and engage with it in a completely different way. Not approaching it with suspicion as a lesser, alien life force, but seeing it as a vast, rich and compatible world with which I can interact responsibly, maturely; something with which I can have a grown-up conversation.

Maybe this is the start of the something I have been looking for as I circled nature for so long, convinced that we have no possibility of a real connection, that we are from different planets. Maybe this is the very simple way to break down all those barriers that have frustrated me before, where I have witnessed other people's enthusiasm but previously found no possible way to replicate it.

Questions remain. I have become enthused by the words of a poet and novelist. I haven't felt anything first-hand. I haven't had an organic experience with nature. There has been no evidential change. It is all fictional rather than gritty and real at the moment. And once I get past the poetry, it is still approaching nature through human eyes and ears. What about approaching nature on nature's terms?

I still have to get through the sense that I am stuck on human beings. That they are overwhelmingly still the prism through which I see everything – that human is somehow higher than nature, a vantage point to look down on the untamed wildness below. It's clear that I have to undo a lifetime's habits, shed a lot of attitudes. Fundamentally change.

Am I truly capable of that? And not even once or twice; am I capable of sustaining it?

With my tendency to lurch to extremes, I have become swept away with a new enthusiasm, but is that all there is? Only time will tell if there is substance.

Nonetheless, I am enthused, and I have always believed that without excitement, change doesn't have a chance of happening. So, it's a start.

I will keep reading.

※

I don't discuss Hardy with Martin.

We are still struggling to get past, "What did you do at the weekend?"

Besides, we have so much else to focus on.

Our first big summer booking arrives – a source of joy and terror. It is Penny, an incredibly posh-sounding woman straight out of *Downton Abbey*.

She emails Emma and her first question is, "How clean is the house?"

It's a question that will be repeated like a mantra over the coming months.

Cleanliness is clearly very important to Penny, in the way that religion is fairly central to the pope.

Instead of pleasing me, this booking just makes me anxious. I am conscious that more and more eyes will soon be on the garden, looking at the trellising that probably needs replacing, the trees that need pruning, the maze that seems to spread out every time I look at it, the worn patches on the nine lawns, at the million and one imperfections. If ever a garden could be looked at and thought unclean, this, surely, is it.

Penny is just the start. Soon, more visitors will be looking at it all, passing judgement, writing reviews: "Lovely house, shame about the garden."

At least the house *will* be lovely. Emma has already made dramatic improvements, painting some window frames, clearing the guttering, installing a 'Nest', from where the temperature can be controlled remotely, on the landing inside. For the first time, the house no longer lurches, as it did when I was there, between a tropical sultriness and bone-cracking cold.

She has assembled a good support team – plumber, electrician, a pair of local roofers – all the ones I haven't been able to find in 14 years of trying. Vans arrive at regular intervals on the curved drive that leads up from the road to the house then bends round back again via a second exit, and men with clipboards in impressive-looking overalls get out, disappear inside, work their magic, then leave.

Martin and I are well into the reshaping of the garden. Now the lawn at the top where the climbing frame used to be is smooth, and the first telltale green hairs from the grass seed are poking up like the regrowth on a bald man at a hair clinic.

Martin has started showing the innovative side of his character, too. He has created an area where we can dump any leaves and weeds out of sight and dry off and store wood. It existed before, a flat patch of ground about 20 x 20 feet, next to the play area hidden behind the hedge, overlooking The Valley. It was occasionally used before, but Martin has completely reconfigured it, putting a wood-store to the left as you walk in, and clearing the remnants of bracken and branches that used to sit there in an ungainly pile.

He has created some fine gates made from discarded trellising, about six-foot high. They have a little hook on the front where you can put a padlock and a hook out of sight on the other side, where you can slip your fingers round inside and leave the key. They look so good, so perfect. When Martin builds stuff out of nothing, it is a miracle as big as the loaves and fishes, bigger, perhaps, because

Jesus had the help of divine intervention whereas Martin just uses power tools.

How does he do that? How do you make stuff out of other stuff? I have never made anything useful. I made my mum a model of a shark in woodwork at school once. Well, it started as a shark, but then I sawed too much off the nose, so I had to saw more off the back to keep it in proportion, then had to shave more off the top and bottom because it looked like a WeightWatchers shark. Then I started again, because the snout looked a little big in proportion, but I took too much off that, so I had to start again, taking more off the back and the top and bottom. Over the ensuing weeks, as I shaved more and more off, the shark got smaller and smaller till it ended up a pilchard. I made that in woodwork, and a cymbal in metalwork that sounded like a dustbin lid and looked like an omelette; there was a shoehorn, too, that would have been more use as a gynaecological implement.

So, I can't make things. I can't do the most basic things with my hands. Under my control, they are as dexterous as flippers. But Martin fashions things. I want to fashion things. He takes them from being one thing and makes them into others, and it is all done with the same kind of beautiful effortlessness he displayed when turning over the soil.

He often says, "First time I've done that," when he has just worked one of his miracles, or when we talk about building something, he'll say,

"Never made one before. How hard can it be?"

Then he smiles that genuine smile which, even though it is genuine, I can see (given the right circumstance) might well start to irritate, because I want to say "Incredibly hard, Martin. Harder than getting an Oxford degree, so stop grinning."

Because at that moment, my generosity has deserted me. All my best qualities have disappeared. All my noble aspirations. Gone are the sweeping enthusiasms for Hardy and grand notions of nature and reconnecting and doing it with my teacher, my guru Martin, Christ-with-a-spade, my inspiration, leading me by the hand down the path of enlightenment.

For the moment, I am no longer that person, no longer the willing pupil, no longer full of unquestioning admiration. I am a snarling, petty schoolboy who is just jealous because he is so good and I am not.

The new me wants him to fail. The new me wants to hear him say, "It has just defeated me." The new me wants his woodstore to catch fire or fall down in slow motion, bit by bit, as an entire house does in that Laurel and Hardy film.

It's even worse, because I've recently noticed a tendency for him to give his constructions a little false buildup, saying how it's not as good as he would like it and it's just knocked together and he hasn't done it as well as they did on YouTube. And he smiles a twinkly smile as he says this, and it is worse because he is genuine. He is not doing any of this for effect, but he may as well be.

Then of course he unveils it, and it is magnificent, absolutely fucking magnificent – built by angels under the direction of Michelangelo. It glows in the light, and when I am looking at it, I can't stop letting out an involuntary gasp, and it's just the same when I see Martin's new handmade tool store or his garden irrigation system or the five-storey summerhouse he has built from mouldy pinecones and squirrel corpses.

Yet even as the light shines on it and the angels sing, a voice inside me is also just incredulous. How does he fucking do that? How do you just DO THAT SHIT?

"Trial and error," he says to me one day, with that grin – which is really starting to get on my tits.

How does that work? Because, for me, it is not trial and error; it is just error. Over and over again. Till the materials are broken and useless, the tools knackered and I am in A & E in Cromer waiting to be stitched up. How do you get it right, EVER? What makes a human being able to GET IT RIGHT ONCE?

I tell you what – I'll trade you. I will trade you my English Lit A-Level.

I WILL TRADE YOU MY FUCKING INSIGHTS INTO THE POETRY OF THOMAS HARDY.

I JUST WANT TO MAKE A FUCKING GATE!

HAPPY DAYS

July 2010

"Okay, fair enough – just give me a clue."

There is a little yelping sound.

I am standing near the garage, up by the climbing frame and the tennis court.

Wherever the yelp is coming from, it is not near here.

I race off down the path that leads by the side of the house to the road.

"Do it again!" I shout.

There is another, similar yelp. It is definitely closer, but in the vastness of the garden it is still unclear where it's coming from. I stop and close my eyes and try to place it; I really have no idea, but I take the steps down into The Valley.

I look around at the sea of greenery waving lazily in the breeze.

"You're going to have to do it again!"

A third yelp – this time much nearer but also much shorter. It could have come from anywhere. From underneath my feet.

From above my head. Here in The Valley, sounds, confusingly, just seem to swirl around as if from no fixed point.

I look to my left at the bank that rises steeply, a thick carpet of shrubs and grasses, then to my right at a similar wash of green.

It is the second time I've been here; it's the second time I have looked around the entire garden. Still, there doesn't seem to be a sign of anyone here.

I can feel the tiredness in my legs. I have bent down and looked under every hedge, behind every tree, in the woodstore, behind the garage, on the roof of the garage.

"I give up!"

Two grinning heads slowly emerge on my left from up high on the bank. It is Emma and her son, Ben.

"We've just been lying there on our backs."

I shake my head.

A whole army could have been lying there – I'd never have seen them.

We are joined by Romy and Lexy, whom I found on the way round the first time, Romy's long legs peeping out from behind a large grass in the bed next to the kitchen and Lexy unable to stop laughing after I walked in front of her three times as she crouched behind a wheelbarrow.

"You got them!" they both exclaim.

"I think they got me."

It is summer, and the garden is at its most dense. Ferns grow over each other, forming a green quilt. Shrubs swell. Hedges become walls as solid as brick, and in the case of the maze they grow over, joining hands to form tunnels dappled by flickers of light from the sun overhead. Beyond the walls and through the tunnels lie new secret pockets of space, dark corridors and rooms with beds of bare earth and the soft smell of damp grass.

Ben is particularly good at finding these secret hideaways, twisting his stick-thin body so that it disappears behind the trunks of the Leylandii that skirt the perimeter of the house or submerging himself beneath the green surface of the ferns. I haven't been able to find him all day (I am normally the one trying to find everyone because I am so poor at hiding).

The look on their faces when I 'find' him and Emma is that of utter triumph.

We have already chased frisbees around, played tennis, climbed on the climbing frame and bounced on the trampoline; the kids have even built a den inside the hedge at the front of the house, hollowing out a little apartment for themselves with a sitting room, kitchen and lavatory. For lunch, we ate sandwiches around the table on the lawn next to the kitchen.

It has been a fantastic, happy day.

Today, I haven't noticed all the usual shortcomings – the peeling trellising, the rotten wooden branches that have come down around the edge of the tennis court, the unkempt, weedy path, the shrubs that have grown over the edges of the lawns, the beds that are latticed with bindweed, the scruffy lawns themselves, pockmarked with the occasional bare patch of ground and studded with occasional molehills. I haven't seen the work that needs doing, the pruning, the weeding, the edging, the thinning, the scarifying and reseeding.

I have been so swept up in the fun, the joy, the sheer silliness of what is going on in front of them, around them, under them, I have barely noticed the shrubs and plants and trees. Or rather, I have noticed them, but they've looked different, their imperfections faded or somehow reduced, their best features blown up as if under a microscope. It is as if their very proportions have changed. As if they are different shrubs and plants and trees to the ones I have been living with.

Not only is my perception of their proportions altered. My perception of what those proportions mean has altered. The unkept lawn edges are no longer irritatingly unkept; they seem harmlessly natural. The hideously overgrown shrubs now just look impressive. Untidy trees appear characterful. The bloated sides of The Valley, a spectacular, eye-catching sea of green.

Details don't register as before, don't irritate like insect bites. Whereas previously I saw a million tiny issues, I now see one happy mass of growth; I see scale and beauty in that growth, my garden a big, loud, fun garden full of personality.

It has felt like a gift today, a real gift.

It is a marked change in our relationship. Often, it's been a battleground, an enemy, a source of head-scratching frustration, confusion and even regret. Something treated with suspicion. Something to be battled, wrestled with. Something strong and bloody-minded. Difficult, obtuse, wily.

Occasionally, I have seen its benefits. I have felt a moment of support. Of calm and relief, lying on the trampoline with Romy after bouncing ourselves to exhaustion as the leaves fall on us from the tree overhead, or doing rubbish handstands on the kitchen lawn, or barrelling down the main path with me pushing her wildly in a wheelbarrow. But those moments haven't been sustained. They have been interludes. A kind of relief, too. Almost a surprise that it could provide something other than an endless series of challenges.

Today has been different, though. I have felt a sense of joy, of exhilaration. Everything has just felt so right, as we have moved from space to space in the garden, as it has opened up to us as a constantly evolving series of delights.

Jenny Uglow, in her wonderful book on the history of British gardening, talks about the transition in the 18th century to a new type of garden, the first landscape gardens; gardens with which you could have a different relationship from before; ones which you didn't just scrutinise from afar, standing on your elevated terrace outside your faux Italianate mansion; ones where you didn't "look down on patterns, as in

Tudor and Jacobean gardens, but actually walked through a series of pictures".

And that is what it has felt like today – a series of delightful vignettes, something unique and amazing in each area to delight and amuse and absorb us, to bring us together.

There is something spiritual about this new relationship, too, as if after a long period of turbulence the garden and I have called a truce and have just decided to set aside our differences – moving our relationship into a new phase. The garden is getting the people it deserves and the family is getting the perfect garden. As if somehow balance has been restored, some sort of equilibrium brought back after the mountainous disruption of bereavement and all the associated negative emotions: doubt, fear, paranoia; the sense of not being deserving; the sense we shouldn't be there; the guilt that I'm not a capable enough steward. All that feels as if, for now, it has just melted away, with the right custodians ruling on the right throne, a family once more for a family garden.

Above all, it feels like progress, a step forwards. As if the family and the garden have moved on – together. At one with each other. No longer arguing. No longer in opposition. No longer worried about each other. Today, the garden is my friend.

❦

It is starting to get dark now. With no streetlights and no lights from other buildings, the garden quickly descends into gloom before lingering in a deep blue half-light for another two to three hours, then slowly, almost imperceptibly sliding into pitch darkness.

We are sitting round the firepit as the flames shoot up into the sky. The garden is a series of shadows that surrounds us, its soundtrack a patchwork of occasional sounds, the snap of a twig from the fire, the childlike yelp of a muntjac deer.

We have eaten our tea – burgers cooked over the flames, sizzling and fizzing. We have toasted marshmallows. Told tall stories. Told bad jokes. Now we have fallen into silence, transfixed by the flames that continue to lick and spit then disappear into the black sky.

It feels as if we could be here for ever.

Suddenly, Romy and Ben leap to their feet.

They put their music on and, as Emma and Lexy and I watch, they start to dance – it's a treat they have been secretly working on.

All you can see are the stars and the dancers beneath them, dark figures in front of the orange glow of the flames – in perfect harmony, like brother and sister, no longer victims of family tragedy but happy and relaxed.

Just dancing.

In this vast dark bowl of a garden.

CAGOULE

March 2019

"I am after a waterproof, er... a sort of cagoule."

I am on the second floor of one of those mountain outdoor tent specialist stores where everything smells of canvas and damp. There are hoodies, jumpers, ski jackets, ski trousers, fleece jackets, walking boots. There is camping furniture, camping lights, sleeping bags, tents, backpacks, water receptacles and cooking stoves. They are on either side of me in piles, on racks, on the floor, hanging from the ceiling above my head. The place is so tightly packed, I fear the whole structure of the shop might just collapse. The good news is that, in the event of that happening, there is so much gear around you could probably survive comfortably amid the rubble for up to a year.

The owner stares at me from behind the counter, confused.

"A sort of *cagoule*?" The confusion is replaced by a smirk. "Ooh. We don't call it *that* anymore."

And there is such disgust in there, such withering disapproval, I feel a boiling rage inside.

"Oh, really, McFuckety? You don't use the word 'cagoule'? Here in your shitty little shop where I am the only customer? You don't use the word 'cagoule'? I've got the wrong word for the stupid little mac you put on then roll up afterwards? That fucking really important item that matters so much in life. I've got the wrong term, have I? Oh, what an appalling error. Forgive me. Maybe I should go now. Retreat from the world. Go inside my house, numb the pain with alcohol and never come out. Just before I go, pray tell me what is it then, so I may know it for ever more, so I shall repeat it a hundred million times and rue the day I walked into your shop and didn't get it right, oh Great One? Outdoor mountaineering vest? Anti-moisture personnel chest-protector? Or maybe it has a Latin name, CAGOULEX REXUS ARSOLEX!"

Of course, I don't say any of this.

I just smile and do that little half-apology that is acceptable Brit-speak for, "I hate you and want to kill you, but actually let's just agree to disagree."

He wanders downstairs and I seethe.

By the time I have come down, he is standing next to the woman at the front desk, his wife or girlfriend, it seems, and he has obviously spoken to her because he is backtracking in that half-arsed way that men do when they realise they are so fucking wrong it is unbelievable, as if they've just worn Speedos in middle age or declared war on the wrong country.

"What I meant was…" he says. "You know, it changes all the time… these labels we attach to things."

He is smiling again, but with a tiny bit less smirk than before and I know what he means is, "Shit, mate, I didn't mean it. I know I sounded like a madman, but please buy something, and even if you don't, please don't walk out of here and tell everyone that I am a sad, middle-aged train-spotting rock-climbing twat who doesn't know how to sell a cagoule."

※

I am starting to feel frustration – I feel so useless in relation to the job I am doing and it is getting me down.

The garden is like a disobedient child who I've been put in charge of and am having no luck in pacifying. Whatever I try – buying it ice creams, playing games, just leaving it – control eludes me.

Martin's presence makes things worse, as he is a constant reminder of this. He is the really competent parent who, with a simple word or gesture, brings the disobedient child to brook in an instant; the brilliant mum who juggles a full-time job and caring for the kids, while I am the useless, stay-at-home, unemployed dad who drinks too much and can't even put up some decent shelving.

It doesn't help that he always looks perfect. Really crisp and perfect.

Martin wears matching T-shirts and trousers that make him look professional and slick, whereas if I wore the same outfit, I'd just look like an ageing holiday rep. He never seems to look different, either. Even after a full day in the blazing sun, he looks the same. He looks trim. Occasionally, if it is 28 degrees, he will mop his brow and smile, wiping away a single magnificent drop of sweat, but that only adds to his heroic stature, for that single drop of sweat is full of character, it is full of meaning: it shows he is gloriously human. It's like Brad Pitt shedding a tear. As if to say, I may be Christ-with-a-spade, but I am one of you too.

Martin is essentially odourless – any definable smell would separate him from his surroundings, and Martin is all about oneness. I am not about oneness in the garden. I am about one-hundred-and-fifty-eighthness. Out of kilter with my surroundings. Out of place, out of harmony. A eunuch at an orgy.

I look terrible to start with. Because I know that my clothes will get ruined anyway, I (rather defensively) deliberately pick awful ones to wear – a pair of old gym bottoms and a baggy, fading lumberjack shirt. By the end of the day, they both look considerably worse than they did at the beginning, with various holes and stains and sweat patches, and bits of thread and birdshit. (This is also partly to do with my one-hundred-and-fifty-eighthness as opposed to Martin's oneness. While he glides sympathetically around the garden not picking up a mark, I somehow always seem to end up rolling around on the floor like a pissed student on a Friday-night bar crawl.) My clothes didn't fit very well at the beginning, but by the time it is starting to get dark, the gym bottoms seem to have lost all their elasticity and I keep having to pull them up. Soon this is happening so frequently that I don't bother, and simply crouch lower and lower as I am gardening, just about hanging onto them using my thighs like a built-in coat hanger. If anyone caught me at one of these moments, it would look as if I were gardening and shitting at the same time. When I have to walk or move at all, it is too much of a faff to pull the gym trousers up again, as this would involve taking off my gloves and putting down the implement in my hand, so I tend to just leave them there and walk with my legs splayed out to the side like a crab, or someone with appalling rickets.

The shirt, meanwhile, is hanging off me like a giant pair of pants with arms. It too has lost all shape; the buttonholes have got big and a button or two has got lost, so it hangs open in various places. It bears the brunt of the sweating, and I have noticed that underneath the arms and across my back the material has become solid and makes a cracking sound when pressed. The overall effect is messy, bordering on deranged. If I start off the day looking like a tramp, I end up looking like one of those Japanese soldiers who came out of the jungle 30 years after World War II, not realising it was all over.

Because I know what is going to happen, I have adopted a practice of trying to limit the damage by never changing my gardening clothes. Well, only changing them very rarely. This means that they are considerably worse than they might have been had I dropped them in the wash once a day. It doesn't seem to occur to me that cleaning them every so often would improve things. I am very determined that these are my gardening clothes and that they should remain untouched. I have always had very specific roles for my clothes – some are everyday; some are for best. These are gardening clothes. It feels somehow right and appropriate that they should be like this – uncomfortable, smelly. I instinctively feel that this mucky work should have a mucky sartorial accompaniment. Added to which, it seems particularly appropriate that mine should not just be dirty but absolutely filthy. Not just a little tarnished but not even fit for recycling.

It is partly a function of personality. Everything I do in life, I do messily. When I open a packet of rice, I rip it open and the grains fly everywhere. Cereal packets that I use look like they have been attacked by a leopard. When I cook a meal, food ends up on the ceiling. I spill things down my front. I scuff my shoes. I trip over constantly like a drunk, even though I am teetotal. No single item of clothing lasts 24 hours without getting debris on it. My wallet is a worn, tired holdall of scuffed bank cards. Even the cash I carry looks like it has been sat on by a skunk.

I have always been fat-fingered, indelicate, clumsy, rough and impatient. I have never stopped and thought things through. I have never calculated and been precise. I have the patience of a football hooligan.

So, it follows that, when I garden, I should end up more filth-encrusted, more bedraggled and odorous than a pig in a mud bath.

But even my natural propensity doesn't tell the whole story. There is something more deliberate at work that I recognise – not just the vagaries of temperament or some inherited genetic disposition to messiness, but a legacy that I've created for myself: a kind of masochism when it comes to my clothes born out of a very conscious sense of unworthiness.

I am not deserving. I am not qualified. I am an imposter. I don't know what I am doing as a gardener and yet I oversee a vast, incredible garden. There is a feeling of inadequacy, a feeling of guilt there. Perhaps even a need to punish myself for this situation – not just by flogging myself like a pit pony or exposing myself to the humiliations of morons in camping shops, but in the very clothes I wear.

I can appreciate Martin's desire to sport a crisp polo shirt, but if I wore it, I'd be like the kid with the immaculate football kit who has no idea how to play the game – a much sadder version of what I look like already. At least now there is a certain honesty in my appearance.

❧

I do eventually get a waterproof. I buy it from the woman in the general store down the road. She doesn't patronise me when I ask for a cagoule-type thing. It is green and zips up at the front. The first time I put it on outside, I slip and fall forwards. When I get up, the front is spattered with mud and I've ripped the pocket.

I'm actually quite pleased.

MUM

April 2011

I am mowing the tennis court.

I look forward to this.

It is the best bit to mow. It is nice and rectangular. No shrubs to make you manoeuvre suddenly left or right, just a deliciously smooth ride with gentle turns where you double back on yourself and you can see the dark stripe you have just created and the pattern building up, like the rows of stitches when you're knitting a jumper.

My mobile rings. I stop the machine.

"Just wondered how you were?"

It is my mum's voice at the end of the phone. She sounds a little hoarse, but she has for a while now. She is 79 and age has made her tired.

"Oh, I'm fine."

"And Emma? How is she?"

"She's well. It's going well."

"That's lovely."

"We are planning on taking a trip soon, together with the kids. For the weekend."

"Where to?"

"Maybe the Broads. Hiring a boat. Just to get away."

"You need time to yourselves. So important."

"It'll be the first time we've really done a trip like that. All of us together. Both families."

"Well, she sounds lovely. I'd like to meet her. Will I get to meet her soon?"

"Of course."

"I'd like to do it soon."

"Yes. Of course."

A beat.

"Mum, is everything okay?"

A beat.

"How was the filming?" (*I've just been away making a TV pilot.*)

"The filming went well in the end. Nerve-wracking at the time."

"You had such marvellous people in it."

"And they were so nice too."

"Meant to ask you, what was that name of that actor?"

"In my show?"

"No, from years ago. I was trying to remember the other day – he had a very round face."

"Er, no idea."

"Round face. Rosy cheeks. He was in that film with that other woman."

"Which woman?"

"Dark-haired woman. She drank a lot."

"Don't know."

"You do know. Dark hair. Welsh."

"I really don't know."

A beat.

"You do... She was in that other film... with the thickset chap."

"No idea. Honestly. Absolutely no idea."

"Oh. We spent all afternoon trying to think of his name, your dad and I."

"I can see why."

"We still didn't get it."

A beat.

"What happens now with your script?"

"It gets edited. Goes to the powers that be. Hopefully they commission a series. I'm just trying not to get too excited. Could be a year or two before it's on screen, at best."

"Hopefully I'll be around to see it."

A beat.

"Mum?"

"Yes?"

"Are you really okay?"

A beat. I can hear a big intake of breath from the other side.

"I've got cancer."

UP ON THE RAILS

March 2019

"Where is it? I need it!"

I can hear the desperation in my voice, strangled and high-pitched.

My ride-on lawnmower, my most vital piece of gardening equipment, has broken down.

It couldn't be a worse time. We're well into March now, and the garden is waking up as if it is late for a meeting and racing around throwing on its clothes. The grass is in a competition with itself – which lawn can grow fastest. There are nine lawns and no ride-on lawnmower and three weeks to go before people will come and stay. Real people paying money. Real people expecting the grass to be cut.

Emma is galloping ahead with the house – she has just repurposed a kid's table that was in the garage and put it in what is now a kid's snug with a TV and a Wii and a host of charming little items on shelves – a geometry set, a couple of indoor games, books, a tambourine and a miniature globe. It is cosy and stylish, timeless and contemporary.

She has certificates for all the electrical appliances, oil tanks have been filled and she has bought and installed an alarm for the swimming pool. She has got new lamps for the rooms and bought nameplates for the bedrooms; we've decided on a literary theme and dedicated each one to my favourite Norfolk authors – Patrick Hamilton, Lucinda Riley, Rafaella Barker, WH Auden, DJ Taylor and Elly Griffiths.

The closer the deadline gets, the cooler and more relaxed Emma seems to be. She is not just multitasking, but multi-multitasking, ear clamped permanently to her phone as she paints, cleans, dusts, builds flatpacks and unboxes new cushions.

She is even unruffled when Penny gets back in touch again.

"How many times is the house cleaned?"

"It is cleaned once before and again after."

"Is it cleaned thoroughly?"

"Yes, it is cleaned thoroughly."

"By professional cleaners?"

"By professional cleaners."

❧

I am speeding up, getting more frenetic. Today I am fretting even more than usual, because time is running short and the one thing I desperately need is sitting immobile and useless in a workshop about half a mile away.

I knew as soon as it happened, a sharp right-hand turn as I always do round the big shrub in The Valley, the shrub that has been dead for years but still looks quite impressive in a *Day of the Triffids* way, so I keep it (that, and the fact that it would be nearly £800 for a replacement).

"Arrggh!"

There was a bump and a horrible clanking that went right up the machine like a knight in full armour going round in a spin dryer.

I'd driven over that root again, the one that hides itself beneath the surface but just seems to rise up like a malevolent tripwire when it hears the lawnmower.

Not again. This has happened before. This has happened so many times that when I ring up the garden machinery store, as soon as I say, "Hello?" they jump in like an overfamiliar hotel receptionist.

"AAAAHHHHH, Mr Gorham!"

Broken blades are just one chapter in a catalogue of mishaps. I have ridden over the edge of one of the lawns and dropped several feet onto the gravel path below, blowing one of the tyres. I have reversed into a tree stump, knocking the back fender off. Once, in comedic fashion, I somehow managed to snap the brake cable and drive into a hedge.

The lawnmower is frighteningly heavy, so I feel I have some excuse. It takes more than one person to push it, preferably three. I once accidentally rode over a hedgehog – already dead, I hasten to add – and afterwards it was so flat it looked like a photo of a dead hedgehog.

Despite the frequent accidents, I like my ride-on lawn-mower. In fact, I love it in many ways, despite the fact it is so heavy and unwieldy. I like it because, when I am on it, I feel in control. Of course, I am not really – hence the accidents – but I have the feeling I am in charge. I can do things. I am powerful. I can make a difference.

Normally when I garden, I am like a sad, lost boy in a massive sweet shop. Now I am the captain of a battleship – though it sometimes feels like the *Titanic*. It's the one time when my relationship to the garden changes. Suddenly I can do things. I can dominate. I can get round all nine lawns in three hours and transform them from unkept, ragged eyesores into pleasing, neat carpets of green. It is not just that those expanses look brighter, cleaner and neater; your whole perception of the garden changes when the lawns are mown. The borders on the sides look less un-even, even though I haven't touched them. The unpruned shrubbery immediately appears less wild.

Martin obviously does the best stripes with his push mower. They are geometrical and lovely. They are perfect. Mine are good from a distance, but up close they reveal inconsistencies in width and the odd dark smudge where I have turned the machine a little too smartly when ap-proaching the corner and churned up the soil with the heavy, thick tyres. I am also good at missing the odd tuft, like the hair on Tintin's head, which, annoyingly, I only ever seem to see when I've got the heavy lawnmower painstakingly back into the garage.

Still, this sort of gardening, for a split second, makes me feel good, feel half-talented. Closer to Martin than I normally am.

So, when I am without my lawnmower as I am now, I am lost.

I get anxious. My gardening self-esteem goes down. I miss its comforting presence, its raw energy. And I worry that the lawns won't get done at all. Which would constitute a gardening crisis.

Lawns to me are fundamental. The building block of the garden. If you haven't got a decent lawn, you have nothing. You can keep your fancy beds and your neatly clipped shrubs; a decent lawn is the foundation. It is Tesco. It is the Guvnor. The Big Cheese. The Chairman of the Board. You can have a scruffy bed, but if there is a nicely striped lawn in front of it, it just doesn't matter as much. You are safe. The bed just recedes into the distance, becomes an irritant, like a single spot on a supermodel.

And lawns have been around a long time. According to Jenny Uglow in her *History of British Gardening*, "the first use of our word lawn from the French 'laund', an open space amongst woods, comes from the 13th century, applied to the smooth green of the cloisters, a place of peace and contemplation". She also talks of the "idea of the level velvety lawn as an essential element of British gardens" taking hold at that time, and describes "the lawn at Westminster being carefully rolled in 1659".

So, I have the weight of history behind me. Which is great – if only my ride-on was working.

So I fret. I worry. I constantly look at the weather. The machine is so heavy, you can only use it when the ground is relatively dry. You need approximately two days clear after a heavy rainfall, and the longer I don't have it then the longer the grass will grow, and once the grass gets to a certain height, you can only trim it, and then you have to go back and do it again or the cuttings will clog up the machine and it is quite possible to get caught in a cycle of bad weather and an out-of-action mower where you never get on top of the lawns again, and they become a permanent eyesore, ruinous to the rest of the garden.

So I watch the weather. I fantasise about when I will get my machine back, at what time of day and therefore when I will be able to use it again.

I ring up the company fixing it. It is next in the queue. They are waiting for a part from Sweden. Why? Why don't they just order a whole lot of parts every summer? They know I am going to need them.

A voice comes back on the line.

"It's up on the rails," they tell me.

It's up on the rails.

When it is up on the rails that means they are looking at it or about to look at it.

So, it's up on the rails. It's up on the rails!

Now. Right now. As we speak.

It's up on the rails.

Good news. Great news. I want to jump up and down and celebrate.

But have they got the replacement blades from Sweden? Just because they have got it up on the rails means nothing if my new blades are still stuck in Stockholm. And what happens if there is a sudden blades strike or a blades shortage or some sort of blades trade war and a blades blockade?

What happens if I never get the blades at all, and my machine is up on the rails for weeks, days, months... forever?

What happens if I can never actually cut the grass ever again? Who's going to want to look out of the window of their holiday rental in Norfolk and see the jungles of Borneo?

But I must keep calm.

It's up on the rails.

MUM

October 2014

"Do you remember when we walked up the path in the garden that winter when everything was white – when it looked like a fairytale?"

She is sitting up now. Her eyes are almost closed and to speak herself is too much. But she can smile as she hears my voice – hearing is the last thing to go, they say. The brightness on her face, the smile, is still indestructible, even when the rest of her has surrendered.

Certain images, certain moments are frozen in time – my mum, propped up with pillows, her head tilted towards me, exhausted but still willing, straining for the light. Vulnerable as a child again.

You're never ready for your parents dying. No matter how old they are, no matter how infirm.

The first round of chemotherapy seemed to have worked, or at least delayed the inevitable, and though I knew, a year *on from the first round, that she was finding her second much harder, she seemed to be coping.*

Then I heard of more hospital visits, and more, and suddenly the chemotherapy was stopped and they weren't going to do any more.

One day, I heard she had been admitted yet again and she was going to be in for a while, and that this time "she felt happier being there than at home".

I knew instinctively what that meant.

❧

Now she lies on her bed in an alcove near the door of a ward in a Brighton hospital. It is a decrepit, crumbling Victorian building with peeling walls and joyless, worn drapes at the few windows – it used to be a workhouse and it feels like it.

There are other alcoves all around her with other beds packed in tightly next to one another – dying on the NHS is a curiously public affair.

My two brothers, my dad and I sit round. Mum's frame has shrunk and she looks pale and ruffled, for all the world like a little raggedy doll.

Her chatty cheerfulness has gone; it started to disappear when she was first admitted and since then she has grown progressively weaker.

On recent days, she could still occasionally spark into life, and if you spoke to her then, if you caught that moment, you could connect with a sentence, even just the odd word; you could see the life flood back into her, the years rolling back like the sea.

We talked often of the house and the garden – I tried to describe them in as much detail as possible. I explained what we had been doing in the garden. September had proved an Indian summer – the late-night fires, the camps, the games of tennis, the fun and the freedom.

I took her back through our Christmas walks in the garden. I tried to paint a picture she could see, and from time to time as her eyes flickered and she summoned that smile, I knew I had succeeded.

At moments like these, I couldn't help thinking of Vikki – when I talked to her once in intensive care in Hong Kong, she didn't seem to register, but I remember her heart monitor quickening at the sound of my voice.

Vikki again. Always Vikki.

❧

On this last afternoon, Mum is no longer speaking at all and she doesn't raise her head, but those around her keep talking. She lies there, eyes shut. Still close to us, but a million miles away.

We have been moved from the alcove, kindly offered the privacy of our own space in a small room off the main reception area. There, we play her favourite music – Frank Sinatra and Uncle George Shearing – and try to create a last, comforting place for her and us. The loving mother surrounded by husband

and sons – her boys. That's all it comes down to in the end. A single room and family. Nothing else matters.

Such a strange thing, waiting for someone to die – we all have to do it and yet no one tells you how to do it. With Vikki, in the strictest sense we missed the moment – she had died before we even got back to the hospital from the hotel – so this is the first time I have been truly present at such an event.

We speak, but it is exhausting, wanting to say that thing. The right thing. The perfect thing. Might this be the last thing we say to her? How to capture the moment. How to wrap up the most perfect thought in the most perfect form. Yet how can I even approach that idea? Last words. The very last words. Ever. It is too much. Still, you try. Still, you are desperate to use the moment. Silence seems like a crime.

In the end, none of it matters. You are just there – just witnessing, just being; when everything else is stripped away, and there is just love and affection and history all gathered up into one vast embrace.

The nurse comes in.

"Can you give us a few minutes – we need to turn her."

We shuffle outside and sit on a row of plastic chairs, no words between us now, just the creaking of the chairs as we change position so that our taut, stressed limbs can find a few seconds of respite.

Time hangs heavy.

I think of Hong Kong, Vikki's final hours there. When they told us at the end of our daily vigil at her bedside to go back

and get some rest, adding that they would call us at our hotel
when she was close… They didn't need to finish the sentence.

Here I am again, entering the long tunnel. That is what it
feels like. A long tunnel. Hemmed in. Dark. The light such a
long way away. I can't believe I am here again, at the start of
my grief when I am already deep inside it. As if I have struggled along far into the black and then been pulled back by my
ankles to start again.

Exhausted before I have even started.

The nurse comes out.

"I think you'll want to come through… She is near…"
The familiar space between the words. The gentle whisper
of her voice.

We walk back in and Mum is there. Very still. Barely
breathing. Frail like paper.

We gather round her and time seems to compress; minutes
become seconds; a lifetime becomes a single moment.

Then she is gone. Quietly and quickly. With no dramatic
moment. No big last gesture.

There is a sudden release of emotion from the others. They
weep and bow their heads, mumble words, give voice to their
pain and anguish.

All of them together.

All except me.

I can't cry. I can't make a sound. I just can't. It is as
if I am blocked off from my own emotions. I can feel the
tears, but they won't leave my eyes. I can feel the sound that

should accompany it stuck in the back of my throat, wedged as tight as a rock.

I just can't do it.

First Vikki. Now my mum.

Too much.

Too much grief, too much anguish and sorrow. Too much pain.

Too much for me to get near. To give voice to.

Just too much.

I can't let go. I can't. I mustn't. Letting go would produce such a torrent, it would rip my throat out, tear the room down, blow apart my very soul.

I hold onto it all. I don't let it go. And afterwards, I feel guilty that I couldn't. I feel like a bad son. As if I've denied something to my mum. That last expression of love, even though she'd gone.

So, grief takes its toll in different ways. Punishing us twice over.

※

Eventually, we walk out through the hospital, people around us everywhere. They are laughing. Talking about holidays. The weekend. Their illnesses. Discussing the local team – apparently Brighton are considering a bid for a highly rated centre-half. He's good, though he's unreliable – bit of a pisshead.

Comments. Rumours. Tittle-tattle. Small stuff. Big stuff.

The sun outside almost blinds me as I emerge. An ambulance races past. The bus arrives ponderously on the other side of the road and I have plenty of time to cross and jump on board before it heads off for the station.

The world outside is unchanged, but for the second time, my world has changed forever.

RABBIT

March 2019

I am standing over the slaughtered body of a rabbit and I don't know what to do.

It has been killed by a fox, or maybe an owl, and just left there, spreadeagled on the main path of the garden just up from the road near the house. It has had its guts ripped out and is flat on its back with its body slit open from its neck to the bottom of its belly. It is unavoidable – you can see it as soon as you turn up the driveway.

The garden has been a killing field since we first came here, with dead rabbits, birds, frogs, moles, hedgehogs, mice and a stoat or two, but they've never appeared in quite so prominent a place. Normally they've turned up in the maze, in The Valley, in flowerbeds and a couple of times halfway under the hedges at the back of the summerhouse. Wherever they've been, they've also either just rotted away naturally or suddenly been dragged even deeper into the undergrowth and devoured by some other creature, so my intervention hasn't been required.

Unfortunately, this rabbit is on the main path and very bloody, so it must be picked up. There is only one problem. I can't do it.

I can't bear animals of any sort, dead or alive. I can't bear to touch them, stroke them, pet them, pick them up. I can't bear to feed them or have them wander around near me. I don't like it when they lick or bark or nuzzle or purr or sidle or leap or run or stand still and stare at you. I only like them in books or oil paintings or documentaries.

How do I move this rabbit? I know I must. If I pretend I haven't seen it, when Martin arrives, it will look odd, bordering on farcical, as if I must have been blind or wearing one of those collars you get after a car accident which stops you looking down. If I've seen it and not done something about it, have I just assumed in a kind of grossly patronising fashion that it is his job as my gardening employee to clear up the mess?

I have no choice – I must try to move it myself.

I can't bear the thought of getting a shovel underneath it, because I would still feel it through the handle of the shovel. I wonder if there is anything longer I could use that would mean I don't feel it at all, but I realise that would have to be some sort of crane.

So I change tack, get a long branch and try to flick the rabbit bit by bit in the direction of some ferns that have grown over the path, so it is out of sight – a bit like flicking a hockey ball with a hockey stick. I reason that the moment of contact with the corpse will be so short that I may just be able to bear it.

Unfortunately, the corpse is flat and, unlike a ball, doesn't really roll very well, so I only manage to flick it a few millimetres at a time, and at the point of contact where the stick meets the 'ball', I can still feel it, of course, so I have to stop anyway as it is making me gag.

I then try getting a shovel and digging round and underneath the corpse without touching it, creating a bed of gravel on which to lift it up. But when I get right underneath it and prise it up, the shovel shoots into the air and the corpse leaps off it and lands back down again on the end of it with a thump, and then I realise it isn't just contact that sends me into spasm; it is seeing the bloody corpse move like that. So I have to put the shovel down, tip it up, then let the rabbit and the gravel on which it is sitting slide back into its former position on the ground.

Then Martin arrives.

Now it is really difficult. I don't want to look like a wuss, but the fact that I don't want to touch it makes me look like a wuss, so I want to explain to Martin the very good reasons why I feel the way I do about animals, which will at least make me look like less of a wuss or at least a kind of wuss with a better reason to be a wuss, rather than just being a wuss out of nowhere.

But then it's hard to just plunge in and explain the reasons, because the reasons are complicated and long-standing and I don't really know Martin yet, and we still haven't really got much beyond "Good morning", certainly nowhere near Thomas Hardy, and I don't want to blurt the reasons out because it might make me appear not so much of a wuss as a complete nutter, and it might scar our relationship and we are going to be working quite closely for a while, and it might make it awkward every time our paths cross – which they will, about 75 times a day – but then again part of me feels I should explain, because they give some context and they are good reasons, because we never had any animals as children, though we did (a cat that went mad and pissed everywhere and an angry gerbil who bit everyone and then got eaten by the dog next door), so this put us all off for a start; and anyway, my mum was terrified of all living creatures, which is why she used to scream every time a friendly Labrador came up to her in the street, which obviously had another bad effect on us kids and is probably the reason why, if a cat jumps into my lap unexpectedly when I am sitting down, I scream like a hyena. And then of course there was this film we were shown at school when I was 12 about rabies and they showed an Indian man dying of it, with froth coming out of his mouth and eyes like black saucers, and although you can be cured, you have to have an agonising 15 injections in your stomach with a syringe the length of a steel girder, if you are lucky enough to have been bitten far enough away from your brain, because if you are bitten closer, then it doesn't work anyway. And they also had a map of Europe showing where all the known cases of rabies had occurred and central Europe was particularly bad, and I remember thinking I am never going camping in Poland EVER – which was a pretty safe bet anyway, because as you can imagine my mum was dead set against camping anywhere just in case she met a stray Labrador, or in fact any other living creature, and anyway, the film clearly had a big effect on me because I can still remember all of those details from 1974, yet now I can't even remember my PIN.

I stare at Martin.

"I think priorities for today, Martin – let's finish off the top lawn where there is some strimming that needs doing and then…" I say, trying to sound vague and non-chalant, my voice suddenly becoming a low mutter "…If you wouldjustmovethisdeadrabbit."

"Sorry, I didn't catch that last part?" he says.

"If you wouldn't just, er, mind, er…"

I then point down and yawn very deliberately, affecting weariness, as if I am just bored with all the mangled rabbit corpses I have cleared with my bare hands and really need a new challenge.

"Shall I move this rabbit?" he asks.

"Yeah… in your own time. No hurry. I am actually in a rush – I've just got to go to the shop."

I try to sound breezy, but it sounds more like asthma.

※

I don't have to go to the shop at all, but I do drive off straightaway. I go home and make a cup of tea and sit down and try to imagine how long it takes to pick up a rabbit corpse and dispose of it if you aren't treating it as some kind of nuclear waste, and I come to the conclusion that, even though this is probably less than an hour, I'd be safer giving it the whole day. This is not as reckless as it sounds – I am also factoring in the time for my embarrassment to settle and Martin's recollection of the whole painful scene to have faded.

When I come back the next morning, I am delighted to see that the rabbit has been removed and, though I make no reference to it whatsoever, I still can't avoid wondering what he thought of it all.

Did he think I was eccentric or mad or just plain scared? Did he have any sense of what my request meant or where it came from? It makes me think how odd this situation is – the two of us working together with no one else around.

We are the only people we see all day, yet we know so little about each other, the workings of our minds, our foibles, our likes and dislikes. We are making sense of each other in short exchanges that contain so much – in the case of the rabbit, a few garbled sentences that betray a lifetime of fear and sadness and hilarity and tragedy and missed opportunity. We are trying to make sense of each other through words that can make, because of their brief and opaque nature, no sense at all.

I wish, somehow, it were different, but I have no idea how to change it.

STRIFE

April 2016

Emma is sitting up in bed, in tears.

I am standing by the window, awkward, ashamed, angry. Unable to look at her directly.

From downstairs we can hear the clinking of glasses, the murmur of conversation and the odd burst of laughter.

This isn't the way it was supposed to go.

It started so well – a long-anticipated weekend break to a hotel in Colchester, a chance to get away for Emma and me, with my brother and his wife. Away from the kids and a chance to relax, to slow it all down, that frantic rush of the last few years: cancer, death, bereavement, survival, starting again, the uncertainty, the responsibility. A chance to breathe again, to take in the fresh, clean air.

A chance to celebrate too. After all the early uncertainties of a widow and a widower getting together, after all the stumbling and social embarrassments, the agonies and anxieties of the early days, after all the posturing and pretence, we've become a team. A good team. Plenty of room for improvement. The odd argument. But solid, dependable. In football parlance, hard to beat and moving up the league.

This trip was supposed to confirm all that, a moment when the two of us could get away and survey our achievement thus far; look down on our bright, new kingdom and give ourselves a pat on the back.

It had been a good couple of days. We'd been to Sutton Hoo and marvelled at the extraordinary story of how a woman in 1939 asked a local architect to investigate the mountainous lumps of earth in her garden and found the skeleton of a longship and, inside, the biggest burial spoils ever discovered in this country.

We'd visited Colchester Castle with its quirky, macabre stories of Roman and Iceni conflict, imprisoned witches and executed priests.

And, even on that final afternoon, there was no hint of what was to come as we strolled around the castle gardens – as Victorian as a stiffly waxed moustache with several South African War monuments, a boating lake and a bandstand, ringed with proud beds of rhododendrons, well-tended paths and healthy, muscular-looking trees; a garden for the people, all chest-pumping jollity and brassy optimism.

Walking around such places tends to make me feel a little downcast, as I can't help but compare them with the fraying, imperfect acres I have back at home, but on this occasion, I

*found myself just enjoying the park for what it was. In fact, I
was so chipper that when someone in our party made a jokey
reference to my ramshackle garden, I didn't feel upset or defen-
sive, I didn't feel the need to drop into a grey silence or shuffle
the conversation on. I just prolonged the joke.*

※

*Only an hour before, we'd enjoyed the finest of meals in a can-
dlelit dining room, the four of us, gossiping, irreverent, carefree.
At that point, Emma and I seemed as far along the rickety
road out of bereavement as ever.*

*And then the moment. The single moment in which it all
changed, like a click of the fingers.*

*Emma said something – that's all, just something. A few
words, an observation, something fairly trivial about the two
of us, the state of our relationship – so trivial in fact that I
can't remember any of the words when I come to write this
down. It was a little personal gossip, a revelation of sorts, but
a tiny one, the kind that most people would barely register. All
I remember is that it stung me so much that it burned, then
consumed me for the rest of the evening.*

*It is something I thought was confidential, just between the
two of us. That was the heart of it. That was the issue. She'd
said something in front of my brother and his wife that I had
assumed would never be aired and it felt like some sort of shock,
almost a betrayal of what I thought we were.*

I didn't say anything at the time, just glowered for the rest of the evening. My replies to anything I was asked were short and tight, as if someone were holding my chest as I spoke.

Everyone could tell something was amiss. I am not good at covering. And the conversation after that slowed down and carried a more careful, threatened air, because everyone knew that something was wrong with me, but no one could put their finger on it and no one wanted to find out in any case for fear it might make things worse. Anecdotes fell away. Laughter was forced. The others became effusively over-sensitive – including me in conversations I had no real part in, referencing me when I was clearly a distant irrelevance. It was as if everyone had been walking in a carefree fashion through a wheat field and were suddenly told it was mined.

Eventually, when the chance came to extend the evening, I was the first to suggest that perhaps it was time for bed.

Now we are back in the room, a tearful Emma rightly wants to understand my taut expression, my icy silence. Why the whole evening seemed to plummet like a meteor.

"What's wrong?"

"I am fine," I say, taking a hard gulp of air and staring out of the window.

"No, you're not."

"I am, it's just…"

"What?"

"Nothing."

There is a pause. I know my "nothing" is not going to suffice.

"Tell me."

"*I'm just not used to sharing things like that.*"

"*Sharing what?*"

"*What you said.*"

"*What did I say?*" *she asks, wearily.*

And then I launch into an explanation of the moment, the remark that caused me to burn.

There is a brief pause.

She stares at me with disbelief.

"*Oh, that…You are upset about THAT?*"

"*Like I said, it felt inappropriate saying it in front of other people.*"

"*Oh, for goodness' sake,*" *she says, half laughing, and something about her casualness, her sheer disbelief that anything so trivial could send me into a tailspin, needles me even more.*

"*You are being way too sensitive,*" *she continues.*

"*I am just saying I wasn't comfortable with you saying that in front of them.*"

"*What's the problem? They are family. They are friends.*"

"*I don't care. It didn't feel right.*"

"*It is quite normal.*"

"*No, it's not, not for me.*"

"*I don't see what the problem is.*"

"*I am just not comfortable with it, okay?*"

"*I think you are making a big thing of it. That's the way couples do things.*"

I am fretting at this point. I am boiling inside. I know what I want to say, but part of me is already aware of the difficult place I am going to with this and I'm holding back, afraid.

"No, they don't," I say.

"Yes, they do!" She sounds exasperated now.

I am stuck. The truth is halfway out of my mouth and I can't stop it.

"Vikki and I didn't."

There is an awful silence. As if the silence is jagged and has cut her. I already want to soften the words.

"I am just saying…"

There is more silence. I turn back from the window and see that she is crying.

"Well, I'm sorry I don't do things like Vikki," she says.

"I didn't mean that… I am just saying…"

The end of the sentence trails off.

❧

It is always there, the previous relationship, a ghostly presence. But it feels like an unwritten rule that you never summon up that ghost. Not in this way.

I have done that. In a moment of frustration and anger. Brought it up. When Emma was just being herself. She has committed no great sin and now she has been hit by this juggernaut.

Now, seeing her like this, I instantly regret what I have done. My reaction seems ludicrously overblown. I could have had a reasonable conversation with her about it all without suddenly invoking the spirit of my dead wife. Why did I do it? It seems silly now. Unnecessary. Unhinged, almost.

What am I doing? Am I trying to ruin everything? It feels that way. An act of such crazy destructiveness – it's as if I am deliberately trying to destroy our relationship.

Just as she and I are on an even keel. Just as we have emerged. Just as we are walking into the sunlight. Just as things are going well. Just as we are enjoying ourselves after years and years of struggle.

Is this insecurity masquerading as self-flagellation? Is this some deep-seated fear of commitment? Is this some kind of twisted survivor's guilt?

It doesn't matter. I have done it now. I have hurt her greatly; I have undermined her. Worst of all, in Emma's eyes I now see that it feels as if I have somehow chosen Vikki over her.

❧

People say that when a widow meets a widower, it is a fresh start. That there are no looming spectres, no baggage.

That is only partly true. There are no divorced exes showing up, no troublesome knocks at the door, no bad-tempered phone calls, no ugly confrontations. No former partners turning up with new partners at family events; no awkward looks across dancefloors at your kid's wedding; no embarrassed conversations at birthdays and anniversaries.

You are free; the slate is clean. There is no one around to haunt you. You don't even carry that sense of blame that divorced couples often do – neither of you chose to lose your spouse.

And yet, there are ghosts way more powerful than the living. Scarier. More formidable. Ghosts that you will never defeat.

For dead people can do no wrong. Dead people are perfect. The person who is still here can never compete. They are alive and flawed, and no one can beat a memory. They are fighting something impossible – an idea, frozen in time. Free from all the complication and inconsistencies of being present.

That spectre never goes away completely. It can always reappear, uninvited and unwelcome. You can get as far away from it as you like. You can remarry, have a new family and live for decades more, but your history will remain your history. Bereavement lasts a lifetime. Your past will forever be frozen in its immaculate place.

So, comparisons are inevitable. In your mind, if not out loud. Comparisons between your old and new life and the way it used to be. We are only human, after all. You can't avoid these moments. You can only be open about them and try to understand them. Realise that there are good and bad things about every relationship and see that those comparisons, if sometimes inevitable, are unhelpful and inaccurate.

Besides, ghosts are just that. They are not real and they cannot be the arbiters of truth. You cannot let them make the rules, but you can make friends with them, give them a name even. Only then will they lose the power to compromise the present.

❧

The laughter and the music from downstairs have faded now.

You can hear footsteps outside as people return to their rooms. The hotel is exhausted and giving up for the night.

I go over to the bed and take Emma in my arms. I am distraught at the pain I have caused. She never deserved this.

"I am sorry. Really sorry. I didn't mean…"

"I know," she says, and for the millionth time she understands.

We embrace and, in that quiet moment as we touch, two bruised souls feeling each other's sadness, all is forgiven.

A CREOSOTE LIFE

March 2019

Closing in now. A couple of weeks till the first arrivals.

The days are passing quicker and quicker, even though they are getting longer and longer. I wake in the night with lists in my head and, without leaving the bed, wander around the garden, seeing sprawling acres of untidy hedge, tatty lawn and weeds everywhere. I see the faces of disappointed guests. I see the negative reviews. I see the whole project limping along because of it. I see bookings tailing off and no way of paying the mortgage. Some nights, I don't get back to sleep at all.

I must press on; I can't stop. Some jobs in the garden are complete now, though too few. Today I hope to complete another.

The summerhouse – a small, sweet, wooden Swiss-style chalet with a sloping roof – stands at the far end of the garden, on the right of the tennis court. Somewhere for kids to play in; somewhere to store the outdoor games, the racquets and balls. Inside is a bare single room, on the left a tiny wooden staircase leading to a miniature mezzanine, room for a couple of seven-year-olds to spend a thrilling, if freezing night or two in sleeping bags. I have already cleaned out ten years' worth of dirt, a choking yellow cloud of dust and cobwebs that have thickened over time into stretchy bands of elastic white wisp that cling to the joists like an old person's fingers. I have cleaned and repacked the tennis racquets in their sleeves, painted the interior a cheerful cream colour. All that is left is to burnish the outside to make it look younger, like a car salesman after a sunbed.

❧

The man in the shop has long greasy hair and is wearing a leather jacket. His expression says it's beneath him to serve me, or indeed anyone; as if this is in fact just a stopgap, not his real job of film producer or rock star.

"I want some creosote substitute," I say, repeating the phrase Martin taught me, but because I don't know what I am talking about – because I am just repeating something I've been instructed to say – I sound awkward and mangle the words a little.

I am praying the man doesn't ask me a supplementary question about creosote substitute, because I know I won't be able to answer it and I hate asking for something when I don't understand it.

"Over there."

He waves his arm airily to the right, but it is quick and dismissive and I barely catch where he is really pointing, so I walk in that direction, but very slowly, like someone stalking a deer, looking hard to either side on the shelves for anything that might resemble it; I don't want to have to ask him again.

Fortunately, I see the words "Creosote Substitute" on the right-hand shelf and stop.

"We have dark black, or brown, or light. The light looks dark," he calls out.

What does he mean, "The light looks dark"? Why isn't it just called dark? If the light looks dark, how dark is it? And what happens if I still want light? Is the brown light? Or is the brown dark? Or is the light dark but just less dark than the brown? Or the brown lighter than the light that looks dark? And how do I know if I want light or dark anyway? I just wanted creosote substitute colour. Is creosote substitute dark or light?

He doesn't say anything more, so I decide to go for the light just because I want to get out of the shop as soon as possible. I walk towards him, and I pay for it, and he waits until I have paid, and I am gone halfway out the door before he calls after me, "Don't you need something to put it in?" in a smirky kind of way (he is clearly related to the bloke I asked for a cagoule).

To which the answer is, yes, of course I do, and from the tone of his voice I think he knows that too and is milking the moment. I hate myself for looking like such a lummox. I hate myself for being embarrassing and not knowing everything there is to know about creosote substitute because part of me thinks that I should know about it, like I should be able to dig and turn over the earth like Martin and wield a hoe so it's not like a stick of poison ivy; like I should be good at building things with a hammer and wood and nails; like I should be able to fix cars and drive bikes and hang out with the guys and shoot the breeze, and be strong and silent, not prefer to discuss architecture and '50s jazz and poetry, and be liked by some women because I'm in touch with my feminine side.

I can feel anger burning my cheeks because this tiny encounter, at least in my mind, just confirms where I am on the macho scale, which is in many ways barely registering, or at least, somewhere down at the bottom with the wuss brigade.

Which isn't right. Well, maybe it is partly right, but it's not totally accurate. The architecture I like is brutalist architecture. I play the drums. I once hit Steven Capel in the second year at school – a good shot, on the chin. I spent a summer going clay-pigeon shooting (okay, it was *laser* clay-pigeon shooting but then it was in a built-up area). I am a mix, but this is all wrong. I am giving him the wrong impression and he is taking it, somewhat eagerly.

That's it. It's HIS fault.

He's to blame – for bearing witness to my discomfort. For not only bearing witness but for maximising it too. It wasn't just the initial smirking when I arrived; it wasn't just the airy, dismissive wave of the hand when I asked where the creosote substitute was. He had to wait, didn't he? He had to wait till I was nearly gone. Until I had to do the slow walk of shame all the way back to him to ask for something to put the creosote in.

I can tell he is enjoying the moment, because when I get to the till he really, really smirks this time; the smirk goes so far round his face, it's as if his head is about to split open. Then he says, "Trays are over there," and does an even airier wave of his hand that could mean the trays are stacked on the right or the left or they are stuck to the ceiling.

When I return with the tray and pay for it, I walk out as slowly as I can because I still have some pride, though I can feel my back burning.

I fully expect him to shout out at any moment, "So long, you big, useless, architecture-loving jazz wuss," but he doesn't.

❦

Creosoting is the process of vacuum and pressure impregnation of wood with hot creosote oil. Creosote oil is a quality preservative made from the distillation from coal tar; the tar itself is released during the coking process as part of the high oven process during the production of steel. First used in the treatment of railway ties for the Philadelphia and Reading Railroads in the early 1900s, it was banned when various studies showed it to have defined cancer risks, hence the introduction of creosote substitute that acted on wood to protect and preserve it, like creosote, and improve grain definition while being less harmful (caldersandgrandidge.com).

I looked all of this up when Martin told me to get creosote substitute rather than creosote. What I didn't realise was exactly how similar the two are to each other – not only in what they do and how they feel when you apply them on to the wood, but in how they smell.

That was something that really shocked me when I got back home, opened the tin and started painting. I hadn't encountered that whiff for a while. I'd forgotten how powerful it was. Not just the sticky, cloying, sweet odour itself, but the way it still has the power to scramble my senses and jolt my whole being right out of its stride; the ability to lift me up with one nauseous inhalation and plonk me down somewhere else altogether.

Back to the '70s and Sunday afternoons. Visits to my grandparents in Polegate in Sussex. Lives lived out in rows of bungalows with neatly trimmed lawns. In well-kept tomato patches and creosoted fences. The Seekers playing on the record player, not too loudly. Grandpa not moving from his armchair. Grandma shuffling around in fluffy slippers, bringing in trays of fish-paste sandwiches.

Retired lives. Slow lives. Weary. Unfulfilled. Waiting. Seeing it out. All of that in the thick, pungent, cloying smell of creosote substitute – the odour of the end of the line.

As I dip my brush in the smooth brown liquid, the smell gets stronger as I paste on more and more. As the slats go a dark honey colour – he was right about the fact that the light looks dark, bastard – I can gradually feel a gloom envelope me like a cloak.

I feel grey. I feel flat. I feel I'm in a kind of despair.

A creosote life. This is what my life has become.

A creosote life.

I feel trapped. Lifeless.

I panic. I attack the job, slap on the liquid faster. Try to shake myself loose.

I refuse to be a middle-aged bloke creosoting a summerhouse.

Forget it – that's what you are now.

Fuck. How did that happen?

That's life.

But it's not my life.

Newsflash – it is now.

But where's the rock 'n' roll?

Shuttup and creosote.

This wasn't in the plan.

Neither was arthritis, but that's on the way too.

But I've been primetime on NBC!

That was then and this is now.

I don't want NOW, I want THEN.

So you can time-travel, can you? Come off it, you can barely use a shovel.

But… creosoting?

Moan, moan, moan. Just embrace it.

I don't want to embrace it. That's like dying.

No, it's just accepting what you can't change. Besides, who gives a shit about the fact that you've been primetime on NBC?

I do.

Well, no one else does. Just paint the fucking summerhouse.

⁂

I can't continue for the moment, my head is too full, so I sit inside it, on the small ladder leading up to the mezzanine and stare at the wall, trying to unpick it all. Trying to understand.

After everything I've been through – the bereavement, the upheavals, the pain, the stress – I obviously don't now have some huge, generous, relaxed perspective on the world and my role in it. I haven't been magically altered by my experience. I haven't been improved. I am just as petty and egotistical and self-indulgent as the next person. Time has not renewed me. I somehow imagined that it would only take some distance from the past for a new clarity to emerge, like a dawn Norfolk fog lifting on a sunny spring day. It clearly hasn't, and that makes me surprised and vaguely disappointed. Did I expect more of myself? Maybe.

Definitely.

Who do I think I am? That I am better than this? Better than gardening?

The cycle of gloom and blame goes around in my head – a frustrating, swirling whirlpool that is in danger of dragging me under. A perfect storm has been unleashed: all the tiredness from the past, that long deep exhaustion I have never got over, the disappointment and frustrations at the present and then the worries about the future. I am drained mentally and physically, and worried about finishing the garden and whether I can help make the rental business a success, but I am still not getting to grips with nature or gardening or any of it; still unable to handle simple things, whether they are basic gardening skills or idiots selling me cagoules or creosote substitute. All I can do is pretend that everything is somehow failing me, rather than the truth, which is that I am failing it.

Where to go from here?

I can't stop, but I feel like I can't continue.

PHOTOGRAPH

February 2017

I am having my photo taken in the garden by a national newspaper. I have written an article to go with the book I have just written about my life with Vikki; about losing her and my attempts to rebuild my life afterwards with Romy.

'How comedy helped me through my bereavement' is the title of the piece, not as crass as it sounds, and they want a picture to accompany the words.

The photographer comes on a cold, late February morning, so the garden is bedraggled. The beds are messy and full only of little green weeds that tattoo the dark brown earth; the trees are empty and starved; the grass is a little too long and unkept, as it always is in late winter when it is still too damp to do the first cut; there are leaves in untidy little formations all over the ground and fallen twigs litter the scene. Everywhere you look it is chaotic, colourless, stale-looking – like a uni student's bedroom.

We start off in the far corner of the garden, where the edge of the grass meets the hedge running along the road, underneath a tree that will be handsome with blossom soon but for now looks stark and bare. The photographer seems pleased with this location. He particularly likes the way the light plays on the trunk of the tree, so I lean rather uncomfortably at an angle of 70 degrees against the bark as he stands 15 feet away, crouches slightly, lifts his camera up to his eye... but then lowers it.

He takes two paces forwards, raises the camera once more and holds it a little longer but then lowers it again.

He looks back over his shoulder, briefly scans the garden to his right, raises the camera, then stands completely still as if he is about to take the shot.

There is another pause.

"Right," he says again.

Then lowers the camera.

"Hang on. Could we just have a look with you behind that tree?" he says, pointing to a tree to his right on the adjacent lawn, the one in front of the house.

So, we move positions from this lawn across the gravel path onto the next one and I lean again, against the new tree, at the same angle, and he crouches and looks through his camera again and holds it as if it is absolutely certain now that he is going to take the photo.

"This is it," he says.

There is another, even longer pause.

Then he lowers his camera and looks to his right yet again, lifts the camera, lowers it, sneaks another glance to his right, raises the camera once more, holds it still and looks as if he is really, really, REALLY going to take my photo this time.

Then he suddenly lowers it again and says, "Could we try you over there?" and he points to The Valley.

❧

In this way, over the next half an hour we gradually work our way round the entire garden until we are back on the very first lawn, just in a different position, with me leaning at a different angle on a different tree.

It feels odd after all the false starts. I've had too much time to think about it. How should I stand now? How should I look? I wonder what sort of expression I should be making. I can't smile, obviously.

Should it be a grief face? What is a grief face? Maybe it is just my natural face now.

I worry that with all the delays, I have lost touch with my real feelings. I can't find them. I can only find the representation of them, the lean into the tree, my melancholic tilt of the head, the tight downward turn of the lips. I worry about the setting: the wasted garden, the leaves on the ground. That everything will look artificial, self-conscious, fake, secondhand and cliched. 'Portrait of a grieving man.'

"Yes," says the photographer finally. "I think we got it."

But what have we got?

❧

Three days later, he sends me the photo and I don't want to look at it.

I put it off for hours. I play with the attachment. I move it around. I save it, but I don't open it.

Finally, in the afternoon, as the shadows are poking long fingers through the window and into my study, I pull it up on to my screen.

Whatever my panic at the time, I needn't have worried about fakery or pretence or appearing self-indulgent or cliched. The photographer has done a brilliant job – all that agonising was worthwhile.

It's there, just there, inescapable and way too visceral to be denied: in my pale complexion; in the purple smudges under my half-closed, battered eyelids; in the ghostly shadow I make on the rutted, mossy bark of the tree, a shadow that seems to be haunting me.

It's there in the dead carpet of leaves, the line of small, starved copper beech plants in the background that have failed to blossom, the horizon that seems to fall into the skyline not with a luxuriant flourish, but as if it has just collapsed, exhausted and unable to continue. In the way that the background somehow seeps into me and I disappear into it, as if we are one. One world, one empty ravaged universe.

I couldn't disguise it even if I wanted to.

Grief and loss.

THE HOSE RANT

April 2019

My existential creosote gloom lifts – I would like to say this is due to a profound realigning of my understanding of the world, the result of some great insight on my part and a profound acceptance of my environment and my place in it, but in truth it's because there is no longer time for existential creosote gloom.

Every minute of every day is full to bursting and my brain is now solely geared towards action; it's stuffed as tight as a Duke of Edinburgh rucksack, full of lists, reminders, questions and ambitions. As I am doing one task, I am thinking of the next or the one after; there isn't the space to think beyond that.

We are quickly approaching deadline. It is measurable now. Not some distant date in the future, but a real day – the Friday after next.

Emma has finished the house. It sits there gleaming and perfect. An incredible show home, a perfect Instagram picture: fluffy white towels immaculately arranged on crisp beds; spotless kitchen surfaces that bounce the light around as if it's a tennis ball; windows so clear they are almost not there. Everything hoovered, ironed, pressed, cleaned, washed, rinsed, dried and painted into a brighter, lighter, neater version of itself.

There are just a few extra supplies to arrive – a fresh set of pellets for the coffee machine, some backup candles, spare towels and household cleaners. I don't think Emma has ever run out of anything. I imagine her as a snotty-nosed child, the only one in class with extra tissues or always having more Rolos when you thought it was her last; I could even imagine her, in a moment of extreme foresight, having backup stores of bogies to pick and lick.

She now spends her days on her laptop, adding detail to the rental website, explaining all the house rules and quirks: not to enter the greenhouse where some glass panels have fallen in; not to jump headfirst into the pool; how to get a caterer in; what to do if you have a power cut; not to be alarmed when you see deer wandering outside while you're having your breakfast in the dining room and please, please don't flush sanitary towels down the loo – they will block it.

Penny has been in touch again – she is still worried about the cleaning situation.

"Will the place be clean ENOUGH?"

She doesn't think she has been very clear before, but being clean is very, very, VERY important to her and her family.

Emma replies that she does realise that being clean is very important to Penny and suggests they have an extra clean, halfway through their stay.

"Will that be enough?" queries Penny.

So, Emma suggests two extra cleans, which Penny agrees to.

It transpires that, at home, Penny has a cleaner every day.

❧

I am now happy in my gardening role, or at least sufficiently absorbed not to be unhappy. It's as if gardening and I have just agreed on a way of working, a kind of mutually negotiated trust – like two old lags who've set aside past differences and agreed to work together on a final job. I know this calm situation can't last, though. I know from experience that when I garden there is always another negative emotion queuing up like an eager autograph hunter to take over from the previous one, but I try not to think about it. After all, I seem to have little control about when it will appear.

Sure enough, it arrives on the second to last Tuesday morning, and it happens in the space of minutes. It is a small thing and a massive one at the same time, like all my negative emotions around gardening. It starts in a single tiny moment that quickly snowballs, gathering up all my other frustrations with it until it is an avalanche, and it rolls down the mountain and sweeps me off my feet as I rage and curse with no idea how to stop its progress.

Hoses have been around for centuries. The ancient Greeks used the intestines of an ox to squirt water, but though the intestine was flexible, it didn't last long and had to be replaced fairly quickly. The Dutch engineer and inventor Jan van der Heyden used leather stitched together to make the first manufactured flexible hose in 1672, but though this was much more durable, it was also extremely heavy. Other materials that were used to make hoses included sailcloth, canvas and linen, but they had similar problems. It was only in the late 19th century, with the introduction of rubber to this country, that things really changed. The Industrial Revolution also played its part, both in terms of advancing manufacturing techniques and creating the possibility of mass production. Twentieth-century developments such as manmade synthetics, especially PVC, continued the evolution along with processes such as vulcanisation. Hoses today are made from rubber or vinyl or a mixture of the two. They are durable and flexible and can withstand enormous water pressures.

Right now, it is 2019 and I am not concerned with durability or flexibility or pressure per square inch – I am just trying to hook up two hoses to each other with the bits you get in the plastic packet; the one that says 'hose bits' on the front.

That's all.

It doesn't sound much, compared to what the ancient Greeks must have gone through, and yet, considering where I am at this moment, I reckon that hunting, killing and then disembowelling a dead animal the size of a small car might have been easier.

I must join up two smaller hoses so that the new, longer hose will reach the swimming pool from the tap that is on the outside of the kitchen wall – a distance of about 12 metres. It is annoyingly just that bit further than either one of the two hoses I have will reach on their own; I have already tried to get them to connect and have failed.

I have been trying for 20 minutes now. The writing on the packet implies the bits inside should fit, but that's a lie. There are no actual instructions to help me.

There is a springy bit that goes 'ping' when you press it. There is a straight bit that goes into the springy bit, but when you do that, they don't then seem to go into the hose. Yet, if you join the straight bit without the springy bit to the hose, it goes in – but then you can't attach it to the other hose. If you attach the other hose to the springy bit, it works, albeit without the straight bit – but you can't fit that into the other hose either. I should say at this point that there are about four other pieces, but I have already discarded them since they don't seem to fit into anything (although one of them does fit perfectly over my index finger like a splint).

I start again several times. I walk away and have a cup of tea. I even watch an old episode of *Minder*, hoping to have cleared my mind before returning. When I do, I find I'm talking out loud to myself like an American self-help book and slapping myself on the thigh.

Still nothing. I can survive bereavement and bringing up a child on my own, but I can't hook up a hose.

So I go to the garden shop where I bought the packet and I wait until the only other person in there, a 30-some-thing (who in my crushed, increasingly bitter brain is doubtless asking whether it is possible to create a Japanese water garden in a clay soil or how easy it might be to create an entirely new species of redwood tree) has departed, and I say to the woman behind the counter in as nonchalant a fashion as I can, "Is this right?", and I hold it out to her, the springy bit inside the straight bit, and she takes it and, graciously, without a hint of surprise or condescension, looks at it and says—

"Yes."

I am pleased she has added her seal of approval, but when she passes it back to me, I still take it apart in front of her and put it back together again once or twice more, just to make completely sure, as if the very act of doing that might mysteriously make her change her mind. It doesn't. She keeps smiling (although I can see in her eyes for the first time just a flicker of alarm bells and I actually want to say, "Don't worry, I am not mad, or completely thick. I'm the holder of a degree from Oxford," even though that has brought me nothing tangible in my life apart from a lot of abuse from fellow alternative comedians on the same bill at a gig at the Amersham Arms in New Cross in 1985 when I foolishly let it slip). But I don't say anything, because even I know that that moment has passed, and if I said it now, it would undoubtedly prove that I was mad or at the very least weird and distressing to be near.

So I leave the shop and get home chastened, battered and glowing, with a kind of red-raw humiliation, but with a functioning hose-joiny thing and convinced that it was just a fluke last time when I couldn't attach it. I get hold of one of the hoses and I get hold of the plastic insert bit, and I look to the heavens, ready to beat my chest and let out an orgasmic roar of triumph, and then, lo and behold, I realise...

The fucker still doesn't fit.

HOW IS THAT POSSIBLE?

The woman in the shop said I did it right. So why won't it fit? The hosey ends on the plastic bit are the wrong sort of hosey ends for the hose – STILL. It wasn't a fluke last time. The end thing or the prong or the teat or whatever the fuck it's called is the wrong... er, gauge... or shape... or diameter, whatever... I am so pissed off I can't even process what the problem is now, IT JUST DOESN'T GO, OKAY?! It doesn't make ONE THING and I JUST WANT TO MAKE ONE THING! Argghhhhhhh!

And I really try. I try to ram the plastic bit into the hose – in, on, through, between, whatever THE FUCK it is supposed to do – but it doesn't work. I press till the blood leaves my fingers. I try to slit the end of the hose with a breadknife to make it bigger, but still the plastic bit won't stay inside it. I even try to squeeze the end of the hose together just in case there is a way of stuffing the hose INSIDE the plastic bit in the middle.

Jesus H Christ, GIVE ME STRENGTH.

How can that be? Why doesn't the plastic bit go into the hosey bit? It says it goes into the hosey bit. The woman at the shop said it should go into the hosey bit. That is its only function, surely? At least, that is what it said on the packet. I haven't missed anything, have I? It's not sup-posed to amuse or entertain or look nice or be some sort of ancient Chinese fucking lucky charm, is it? NO, IT'S JUST SUPPOSED TO GO INTO THE HOSEY BIT.

Then it occurs to me. Are there different versions of garden hosey bits for different hoses, like there are different types of everything else in this bloody world?

If so, WHY? WHY WOULD YOU DO THAT? Why would you make someone's life extra-complicated by de-signing different hosey bits? Why would you not just say, "I know, let's make his life simple so that he doesn't waste hours of his life that he will never get back, having to work out which hosey bits he needs"? Why would you not say, "Look, life is hard enough. Give the guy a break – his wife died, his mother died, he can't get any more work as a writ-er so he's just downsized, and he can't sell his house now, so he is a full-time gardener and really useless at it, so let's not make things any harder for the poor sap. LET'S NOT FUCK HIM UP WITH DIFFERENT HOSEY BITS!"

All I want is someone to solve this problem for me. Please, just come to my house. I will pay you. Just do it for me. I don't want to touch the fucking hose ever again.

How much do you want? I have cash. I will pick you up and drive you home afterwards. You can take some furniture home too. Some vinyl. I have a couple of nice pictures.

I beg you.

❧

Fuck the hosey bits.

Fuck gardening.

Fuck nature.

REAR WINDOW

November 2017

Nine months on from the newspaper photo and I am looking at the garden, at one of the many backdrops that the photographer really liked but didn't like quite enough.

This time, though, I am looking through the window of my bedroom, as I do pretty much every day, because it is much safer that way – no bugs, no bites, no plants, no chance to slip over, no chance to cut myself on a stray branch or thorn or get stung by a spiteful nettle. Nothing that can disturb my flattened immune system. Such things are important now. They mark out my day as clearly as an electrified fence around a field of cattle – to ignore them is downright dangerous.

For, unbelievably, this time I have cancer too.

It started as a lump in my neck, on the left side. A small but visible swollen gland that you could push around but that refused to disappear. I went to the doctor, who felt it and said there was nothing wrong, but after a month, when it hadn't gone away, I went to a different doctor, who disagreed and ordered a scan.

The source of the cancer was my tonsil, the swollen gland a secondary, so it was already advancing – creeping around my body stealthily like a burglar on tiptoe. I hoped it had been caught in time.

I still hope.

Now I am deep into my regime – thirty radiotherapies and six cycles of chemotherapy at the same time. When I am not at hospital, I am at home, looking out of that window at the garden while the little machine I am plugged into pumps nutrients into me because I can no longer take in food except by means of little bottles of high-protein gunk through a thin tube directly into my stomach.

I have lost two stone in weight. The skin is peeling from my neck in white sheets. My face looks sallow and gaunt. I could be mistaken for a consumptive Russian novelist from the 1800s, a notion which would normally excite me on several fronts, except that now I don't have the energy to be excited about anything.

I am exhausted. Drained. Battered. From my burning throat to the bruises from the needle marks on my arms to the red marks around my nose from the oppressive fibreglass mask that clamps down on me like a vice during the radiotherapy.

The only time I go out each day is when I go to hospital. I don't have any social appointments. I don't speak to others. My bedroom is my everything – my refuge, my solace, my inspiration, my friend.

When I am cocooned in my room, the only connection I have to the outside world is through my view of the garden – the lawn outside that gives way to the path and beyond it the edge of The Valley.

Beyond that is the other side of The Valley, with thick shrubs and miniature firs and towering oaks and elm and eucalyptus trees that dominate the skyline, the sky peeking through their upper branches like a nervous child anxious not to be forgotten.

It is hope. Just there. Where I can nearly touch it – a natural world blissfully unaffected by cancer, by whirring machines, by tubes, by pain, by secondary infections, side-effects and sleep medication.

For someone who is not really interested in nature, I look at it a lot now. I watch the little dramas unfold outside – the squirrel chasing the other squirrel up the tree; the ongoing dispute between two pigeons over who owns the top of the hedge where it bends round and down towards the road; the faint outline of the stately barn owl who sits on the front lawn when dusk settles and lets out its classic Hammer House of Horror "Te-wit-te-woo!" I like to watch the muntjac deer as they wander up the drive and the impressive squadrons of waders that fly overhead in perfect V formations all the way from Canada. And I even enjoy the leaves falling. Sometimes I try to follow a single leaf from the branch as it falls all the way down and I try not to lose it among all the other hundreds heading in the same direction.

I am particularly taken with the squirrels and the soap opera of their lives – their routines, their interactions with one another and the rest of the garden. I become obsessed by the way they dart around, then freeze – they'd be phenomenal at musical statues. How they swish their tails to signify a threat and occasionally let out a cry.

When I read up, I realise I'd underestimated them. As fellow mammals, they are intelligent; they can memorise where they have put a supply of food for a year or even longer and have an incredible sense of direction. They can also apparently recognise people and experience real human feelings, such as fear, happiness and even sadness.

Most of all, I have seen in them an energy I don't possess, a sprightliness that has drained from me. They have an electricity, a zest about them; sometimes when they are not searching the ground for acorns or nuts or plant bits they just chase one another through the undergrowth like demented school kids.

Sometimes, too, they just freeze and stare up at the window when they see my face come to the glass, and we sit there in silence, eye to eye, fascinated with each other.

There is something pure about them; in their stillness and concentration; the way they have mastered their world. Their lives are beautifully purposeful and streamlined, yet they aren't empty. There is emotion and cleverness in their minds, dynamism and energy in their bodies.

❦

So, like James Stewart in Hitchcock's Rear Window, *I spend my time watching, following the stories outside, imagining the background to them, what happens when they disappear or I am asleep. I forget my own dreary reality of constipation and foul tastes and nausea, and escape into these other worlds. And just being there is bliss – like taking another painkiller, one that doesn't dull my mind like the others; one that somehow brings it alive instead.*

When I am taking in the view through my bedroom window, I make all kinds of bargains with it too. I promise to cherish and preserve it in my mind forever if I can just get well again; to never again complain about the small things – the fact that the hedge never stops growing, the fact that the lawns become scruffy, that the hyacinths quickly fade into tired blobs of scrunched-up paper and I need to deadhead them and never do.

I vow to be a changed person. To value nature in a different way. To appreciate the simple joy it gives me. To be a gentler,

*calmer, more philosophical individual. To see myself as I am
– a small cog in a vast natural universe.*

Lots of promises, but can I keep them?

Carl Gorham

THE IMPORTANCE OF
BEING EMMA

April 2019

We are a week away. A week away!

Emma has had the final checks done. The health and safety man has been and given his recommendations. As you walk around the house and garden now, you get shouted at wherever you go. Instructions have been placed on all four corners of the swimming pool cover that say "DANGER. POOL. DO NOT STEP ON THIS COVER". There is a board up next to it with a lifebuoy and a set of instructions that says, "NO JUMPING IN" and "CHILDREN ARE NOT ALLOWED IN THE POOL WITHOUT AN ADULT". In the house, there are signs up over low doorways that say, "MIND YOUR HEAD". When you come into the house, there is a sign that says, "MIND THE STEP" and in the games room you are told in no uncertain terms, "DO NOT WALK IN FRONT OF SOMEONE WHEN THEY ARE PLAYING DARTS".

With the house set elegantly, expectantly and ready for the guests, Emma is doing some last-minute social media, writing sumptuous Instagram posts with bright pictures of immaculate rooms that seem soft and inviting and glisten in their own haze as if existing in a dream. In the bedrooms, the pillows are perfectly plumped and the new bedsheets are as smooth as alabaster.

In the living room there is a throw elegantly slung over a sofa, while on the coffee table opposite the fireplace, where the orange flames from an open fire twist up into the chimney, a coffee mug sits on a carelessly yet immaculately strewn Sunday paper. In the kitchen, fresh flowers of purple and red light up the otherwise perfectly white surfaces, on which sits a freshly baked loaf cut on a breadboard with a scattering of crumbs. The dining room, with its long oak table that seats 14, is elegantly laid with a gleaming, perfectly spaced dinner set and glasses that sparkle like diamonds.

The bookings are increasing. New names and photos appear on the regular printouts that Emma leaves on my desk at home. Real people with names and faces. Preferences. Expectations. Likes and dislikes. Difficulties. Issues. Things they object to. Things they can't abide. Things that might make them go online after they have stayed at the house and say things that will eviscerate the business as swiftly as the discovery of snakes in the kitchen.

Emma seems unruffled, serene even, as she approaches the day of the launch. Still no perceptible quickening of her step. No exclamation. No objects hurled. No despairing wave of the arms.

Her voice remains calm when the plumber points out a watermark on the ceiling of one of the bedrooms and a problem with the water pressure that he can't fix. When a dead bat is found in the cold-water tank and the TV in the upstairs bedroom conks out, she just raises her eyebrows and chuckles.

Her voice is still measured, even when the health and safety officer who suggested that we make the warning signs starts making other ludicrous observations on his return visit, such as the fact that the corridors in the house are "rather narrow". And whereas I would probably have suggested either increasing our public liability insurance by three thousand per cent or possibly even closing off the corridors and adding rope ladders so the occupants could escape via the windows in the event of a fire, Emma, of course, remains completely zen, laughs it off and does an amusing post about it on Facebook.

Somehow, her calmness still puts me a little on edge, though. I know I can't match it and I have long since given up comparing myself in that respect, yet it troubles me, nonetheless.

I am convinced that her panic is out there somewhere, waiting to resurface. No one could just be that serene. I feel that human anxiety – like the seasons, or gravity, or the total amount of the world's wealth – is probably a constant; that there is a certain amount of it out there and that doesn't really change. Even if Emma isn't using her quotient now, I am convinced the rest of it is still floating somewhere in the ether, waiting to be taken up by someone. Maybe by her in a few days' time, the night before the first guest arrives, a sudden terrifying thunderclap of fear, the last 45 years of her ice-cool life all blown apart in one moment of revelation where she finally realises the awful responsibility she has taken on with the business we are opening, then screams, runs barefoot to the airport and flies off to a new life in Gozo.

Ok, I might be exaggerating. It might not be Gozo. But what if she just goes to Bury St Edmunds to clear her head? Even if it isn't the full-blown fleeing-your-life type thing, she might well want to recalibrate for a couple of days and go tenpin bowling. After all, she's only human and even the best people can suddenly snap. She has been so unbelievable, and I worry that no one can be that focussed for that long on one thing – not without a bit of pointless shopping in between.

Which means the burden might suddenly fall to me. I might have to take over. Be in charge. Assume control, at least for a few hours, a day or two – something I haven't ever really considered to this point.

So, what's the problem?

After all, I could do that, couldn't I? I could hold the fort. On a temporary basis. I could step into the breach. Take the reins. That isn't too much to ask, is it? Is it?

IS IT?

Yes, of course it is. Ten minutes in charge would be too much for me. Like putting an ape in charge of guarding a banana stall – the mayhem would be instant. As I've said before, I am impractical, but that's being modest, I am more than that, I am a whole subspecies of impractical – where it is taken to an almost surreal level. Where it takes on the appearance of idiocy. I once wore a suit of mine to the dry-cleaners to prove to the dry-cleaners that it didn't fit me and therefore wasn't my suit (it was, of course, I'd just put on weight). At a posh restaurant I tried to wash some grapes in a finger bowl thinking it was for the fruit. Once I even bought a bottle of wine vinegar, convinced it was wine. Emma, the Princess of Practicality, has clearly been selected by some merciful god who took one look at me and said, "Wow, this Arse needs PROPER help!" The flip side of this mismatch is, of course, that if

Captain Sensible ever leaves the ship, it is sinking faster than a concrete cruiser.

Of course, I've always liked to think of myself as a secret stoic. Someone who on the surface might flap but would surprise everyone and come through on the big occasion. Someone who'd turn into a hero when the Germans invaded. But who am I kidding? I'd be racing around making strange incoherent noises and crashing into the furniture – a cross between Road Runner and Corporal Jones in *Dad's Army*.

With me in charge, it would be mere seconds until it all fell apart. Until the first phone call from the guests saying they couldn't use the Nest at the house. Or the key-box or the cooker. Or they just wanted to know where Gunton was.

What would happen then?

Well, it's not like I wouldn't try, of course.

I'd fight back in my own eccentric, baffling, useless way.

I'd purposely drop the phone. I'd stammer. I'd invent something far-fetched as they do in bad comedies—

"Er, someone's coming to the door now!"

"Oh my God, the wall's falling down!"

"I… can't… breathe… urgh!!!!"

And it might work – it *might*. People could be so confused that they'd have to retreat and regroup. Or maybe they'd decide there was something mentally awry with me and take pity. Or indeed be so alarmed at my response they'd think that having to cope themselves with a sudden flood/house fire/exploding kitchen just might be an easier option.

Whatever the case, it all boils down to one thing.

Emma just can't go to Gozo, Bury St Edmunds or anywhere else. She can't flip out, disappear or recalibrate. She can't delegate. She can't take a break. She can't take a pause. She can't take a breath. She just can't.

She must always be in charge.

Of everything.

Even when she is asleep.

That's the importance of being Emma.

THE FLOOR

August 2018

I am on the floor of the living room. I am hugging the floor-boards, clinging to them, my knuckles white, like a ship-wrecked sailor.

I always thought that people had breakdowns when things were going wrong, but it's not true.

We have just bought our shiny, new, modern home and we have started talking about the renting out of my old one, but we haven't yet set out on that road. I have been given the all-clear from the cancer. I have regained my strength, put weight back on. A lot has changed. A lot has improved.

Yet, at this point, it feels that nothing has changed at all and nothing has improved; that I haven't left the past behind; that I haven't moved forwards or on or even sideways. On the contrary, it feels as if I have gone back, collected up the last 20 years, hoisted them onto my shoulders and then collapsed under their weight.

I can recognise this at the time it happens, even as I am lying there, hardly taking in air. But then, I know this feeling.

I have had brief collapses before, like sudden full stops, and they have always been the same – a period of intense stress, a gradual building of something fairly innocuous that suddenly becomes the focus of obsession and triggers the blowup and then, in a single, spectacular moment, a real physical collapse – an inability to breathe, a dizziness, chest pain and suddenly I am on the floor, holding on.

This time, the symptoms are all there as they usually are, but there is something else with this episode. A sense that there isn't one beyond it.

Before, when I broke, it was a juddering interruption, a momentary loss of balance in my life as if everything were being shaken. It was brief, it was violent, but it somehow always carried with it the shape of its own recovery.

This feels somehow different: something complete, something finished, something not to be repeated. My body cannot feel more torn. My blood cannot rush through my veins harder, or else it will explode out the top of my head like a geyser; my neck cannot be tighter without my whole spine being rammed up into my brain. I cannot breathe less without losing consciousness.

The vows from when I was undergoing my cancer treatment, that I would lead a new life and gain a new relationship with nature and find a new perspective, have dwindled and disappeared along with the illness. I haven't been able to find that stillness, that sense of communion anymore. All that has replaced it has been a fractious, nervous dissatisfaction.

The Floor

The aftermath of cancer, I have read, can often be worse than the treatment, and I have struggled to re-find my place in the world. I am different, but I am the same. I am changed, but I am still me. How do I resolve these things? And what should I literally do now? Should I walk round the world for charity, or go on some carefree hedonistic odyssey? I want to do something, but I don't know what it is. I feel the pressure to appear released and emboldened by my experience, whereas the truth is I just feel shitty.

The spark for my current predicament is, as always, something relatively trivial; my keenness for my daughter to get her applications to dance college in on time – a stressful parental moment, but for most people an everyday concern. But, as happens to me occasionally, it has become something else – a monstrous, bullying preoccupation that dominates my thoughts, rattles my brain, makes me nauseous and deprives me of sleep. It has ceased to become part of the fabric of everyday life and has mutated into an ultimate test of everything that has gone before, as if it is some metaphysical judgement on the value of my entire life.

I have always had a propensity to these occasional moments of implosion. My capacity for obsession, as demonstrated most fully by my 'Thinks', is a rich and rewarding gift, but also has the potential to turn in on itself and trap me in a spiral of self-accusation.

I also have an oversensitivity to the outside world, allied to a tendency to take on responsibility and a propensity for self-blame that has become more than a reflex, more a governing tendency. Add in Vikki's death, the bereavement, the struggle to cope bringing up a daughter alone, the tension of trying to negotiate a new relationship, my mum's death, my own battle with cancer, and it doesn't take a professor of psychology to see me as something of a rumbling volcano, fit to erupt without warning.

I can't pinpoint which problem is most to blame. Whether one issue is underlying all the others. Whether I am just suffering the inevitable conclusions of many years of emotional overload. All I know is I am there again, at the point of collapse, and this episode feels somehow different and seems to mark some sort of end – not just for me, but for Emma too.

She has patiently been through it several times with me down the years, supported me, gently suggested I speak to the doctor, get some counselling, change my lifestyle or pursue some combination of all of these. Each time I have dabbled, felt mildly better and stopped. Ultimately refusing each opportunity. Feeling that I was still stronger, that I really didn't need help, that I could cure myself. That I had cured myself.

Each time, she would shrug and let it go, and things would calm down again for a while before the cycle would repeat itself and the storm clouds gather and she would have to wait for the next dramatic explosion, all the while knowing it was coming; knowing, too, she would have to go back and gently suggest the same things all over again. Each time, I would claim to be more willing than ever to act and try a few more things – a visit to a different doctor or a different counsellor or a different nutritionist – but all of it quickly, and somewhat half-heartedly, before giving up, convincing myself that it had all gone away.

In one sense, I was just too relieved to have got through my collapses to think about them afterwards. I just wanted to walk away and forget they ever happened. In another sense, I would probably have to concede that I was annoyed and frustrated that I kept going round in circles and didn't like that being pointed out to me. I also genuinely believed that things would always get better afterwards. I had an optimism that it was something like a catharsis, something leaving me, never to return.

"You need to get help," Emma says.

It feels like the end now. That even her extraordinary calmness and patience is exhausted. It feels, although she won't say it, that even if I survive, our relationship won't.

❧

I park outside on the uneven, half-gravel, half-mud square at the front. The woman at the appointments desk is talking to the woman at the computer screen behind her about Love Island. *I give in my name and take a seat in the waiting area, my body so tight from tip to toe that I must lower it slowly and literally topple into the seat. (I always, even in the dark moments – especially in the dark moments – think of that line from* The Odd Couple *when Oscar says that Felix is the only person he knows who has clenched hair.)*

I must explain. I must get it right. I must describe it well. I HAVE TO GET IT RIGHT. Times. Dates. I must get the right words. Not undersell it, because that is what I always do. Normally I smile. I'm articulate. I am in control. I play it down. I say I'm fine, but I'm not. But this is the problem; this is what has really got me to this point. You have got to stop coping. Stop coping because you are not coping. Even though you say you are coping.

I realise what I must do. The scale of it. And I can feel the nerves inside me rise still further because I see the size of the challenge. And it feels like the only chance I will get to do this, which makes me tighter still. The only moment. THE moment. The single moment. A fraction of a moment. A window of opportunity. My life on a pin.

The doctor calls me and I follow her along the brick corridor in silence. I take the seat next to her desk. She looks at me. I know it is the time to speak.

I sit. And for a moment it feels impossible to bridge that gap. My doctor. A wet Thursday in Melton Constable. Me. The years of being hammered. My body fit to burst. The explanation just as vast. How do you…Where do you… start?

How do you get from hello to crisis? How do you get from good morning to please help me, I am breaking down?

Then I just start. What has made me start? Doesn't matter; I have just started.

"I am just not coping."

I hear those words.

"I am just not coping."

Then I stop. I have surprised myself.

I have never said these words before in my life.

I have said I am finding something difficult. I have said something is a challenge. But always it has been qualified, measured. Always, I've implied I have somehow been in control.

"I am just not coping."

The words sound so strange. I sound like someone reading out of a manual. They feel unfamiliar, as if I am impersonating someone else. Someone else who is having a breakdown, which only makes me realise once more I am having a breakdown. This is what it is like. The endpoint. When the road has run out. After you have had these moments before, and your body just erupts like a river bursting its banks and you end up at a doctor and it is so dramatic and so undramatic at the same time.

I recite the whole story – the state I am in, the anxiety, the inability to negotiate life – the history. My childhood obsessions, then Vikki's illness, her death, the stress of coping with a young daughter, my mum's illness and death, my own brush with cancer and I can feel it all piling up. I can feel for the first time the sheer weight of it all; the way it has been pushing down on me, crushing me not even just in my broken moments but actually in between, too – covered over, disguised, ignored, but there nonetheless. I can see these stresses piling in on me like people jumping on me one after the other. I can understand what they are doing.

There is a moment, a black comedy moment, when even the doctor winces at the events I describe and it momentarily feels like the 'Four Yorkshiremen' sketch from Monty Python, *as if I am trying to outdo any tale that has ever been told in her room.*

"I'm just not coping."

Now the words feel more familiar, almost delicious. They are the words that have started me. They have uncorked all this. They are my friends, these words. They are trusted ones. They are my rock. I like these words. These words are helpful – like a polite teenager.

"I am not coping." I don't know how many times I have said them, but it doesn't matter. Now I am easy with them, I can fling them round and not care where they land.

"I am not coping."

For the first time I notice how serious she looks. How she is nodding and rattling the keyboard as she makes notes.

"Are you having suicidal thoughts?" she asks me.

"Not in any meaningful way," I say. Because that is true.

"But I am just not coping," I add.

I can't stop saying the words now, like someone who has bought a new pair of shoes and can't stop showing them off.

"I think it may be time for you to have some help," the Doctor says, then talks about chemical imbalances and mood enhancers, and though this isn't the first time I have had the conversation, it is the first time I am relieved to have it again.

I barely remember leaving the surgery, but then I realise I am out in the cool air with a box of sertraline in my pocket and the feeling that something substantial may be about to change.

PARANOIA

April 2019

"How clean is it outside?"

Penny has emailed again.

"In the garden?" replies Emma.

"Yes. How clean is the garden?"

"It is clean... given that it is a garden."

"Is the swimming pool clean?"

"Yes, it's clean."

"But are there things in it?"

"Well, there's the water..."

"Are there creatures?"

"Yes, occasionally – it's an open-air pool."

"What type of creatures are there?"

With her hotel background, Emma is normally comfortable dealing with a whole range of people. There may be awkward, difficult ones in there, as well as pleasant and helpful ones, but ultimately, she feels a level of goodness will prevail – a consensus of the nice. She is as keen as me to get off to a good start and get a decent review, but she is philosophical and equally knows that it is not ultimately in her control.

I don't have Emma's perspective. I have fixed on the notion that any single guest could post a bad review and ruin us. I have not allowed the much more realistic prospect that we will get a variety of responses. I have done what I always do – I have lurched to one extreme. I have catastrophised. And I have catastrophised the catastrophisation.

I know it stems, in part, from my own feelings of guilt about the garden – that it remains an unfinished project, full of rough edges, unattended corners and improvised solutions. Martin and I have actually started trying to hide things now, throwing fallen branches from the trees over the shrubs in The Valley so they disappear from sight; sweeping leaves under hedges rather than gathering them up on the leaf pile to rot down; even roping off some paths from the main driveway down into The Valley with 'No Entry' signs just because we haven't had time to clear them. It's become a garden full of cheats, cons and sleights of hand.

At the same time, I recognise that my perspective is somewhat skewed. I know that I am no longer seeing the totality of the garden. I have lived in it now for months. I am seeing every detail, every imperfection. I cannot see it as a newcomer would – a vast, rolling sea of greenery that runs from your feet as far as you can see, its waves towering above your head and reaching right up in the sky.

I cannot see the panorama. I see it as a patchwork of errors. Even where there has been achievement, I can't enjoy it for itself; I can only see the agonising, sweat-drenched days of labour that made it so.

Yet, despite this awareness, second-guessing our visitors by looking at their picture profiles on social media has gone from being a distraction to a gloomy obsession, at least on my part.

Does a smiling face mean they are likely to be friendly or over-friendly? Does a serious face mean they will be humourless and quick to disapprove? And just because they are in Ibiza having a great time holding up a glass of something fizzy in a hot-tub, does it mean they are decent hardworking folk who just like to enjoy themselves, or wild party animals who will trash the house, push each other through hedges on wheelbarrows and leave turds in the swimming pool?

The reviews. It is all about the reviews.

What will they say?

I have no doubt they will love the house, with Emma's fine organisation and subtle touches, the crisp clean look of the furniture, the soft laundry, the well-equipped children's playroom and the thorough-going instructions that can tell you equally well how to find a shop that sells umbrellas, or why Blickling Hall is one of the finest examples of Tudor architecture in East Anglia. But what will they say about the garden? Especially if the house is good – will that make it worse?

"Lovely house. Shame about the garden."

"Inside great. Outside rubbish."

"The house is a bijou hotel. The garden's like a builder's yard in Cleethorpes."

❧

Time to empty the septic tank. Well, it may not be time, but we are going to do it, just in case. We are into the realms of 'just in case' now. Checking. Double-checking. Being sure – absolutely, doubly, triply sure... It's unlikely, but if it does... Probably won't happen in a million years, BUT.

I have already smelt that familiar smell – that overpowering stench. It could be something and could be nothing. You hit it around the bottom of the first driveway. A sickly, dense odour that clogs your nose and scratches the back of your throat and makes you want to be sick immediately and spectacularly, like they do in cop films when the fresh-faced rookie has been shown a mangled corpse by the cynical, grizzled veteran. You can feel it pulling at your lungs. You can't believe that something that strong can't be seen.

The septic tank could be full, or it could just be a phantom smell. I have had phantom smells before at key times – on Christmas Eve, for instance, when I know I have family arriving and haven't got a chance of getting the slurry men out. It has also happened at Easter and just before the August Bank Holiday – an absolute conviction that the smell must mean that the tank is full and that any second the sewage is going to come bubbling up from the ground like a brown Vesuvius. On each occasion, though, when I have finally got the slurry people around (they are rather delightfully now called 'refuse engineers'), the tank has been half empty and I've been forced to reflect on the power of the human imagination to deceive. On each occasion, too, I have vowed not to let myself be tricked again, a promise that I have managed to keep only until the next major festival in the calendar.

I could always just take the cover off, of course, and have a look myself, but I am nervous of doing that because I am not only afraid of what I might find, I am also afraid of some sort of disaster. Some time ago, I read in the paper about a couple of Irish farmers who, while investigating a septic tank, fell into it and drowned. I also don't think I can ask Martin to do it, either – mangled rabbits are one thing, but asking him to check out my stools would, I feel, mark a new low in our relationship.

I manage to get some refuse engineers to visit, three days before the first guests arrive. A large lorry with two blokes in the front pulls up in the road at the bottom of the drive. A tall man gets out, wearing jeans and a T-shirt, unrolls a hosepipe that is wound round the side of the vehicle and drags the hosepipe up the drive and across the edge of the front lawn till he has reached the top of the septic tank. He then lifts off the top of the septic tank and drops the hosepipe inside, walks back towards the lorry, stops, then signals to the other guy in the front of the lorry, who switches on the pump and the hosepipe starts jerkily inflating and straightening like someone getting an electric shock. The man in the driveway walks back to the septic tank and peers in, while the slurry is emptied from the tank down the pipe into the lorry. When the septic tank is empty, he walks back to the driveway, then calls out; the engine is switched off and he walks back to the septic tank, pulls the pipe out of the tank, drags it back to the lorry, then winds it back up on the side. I have been watching all this from an upstairs window inside the house (to be outside at this point in any kind of proximity would be intolerable given the smell).

Afterwards, the man walks to the front door and gives me an invoice with a little dark brown stain in the corner, which I must assume is poo. He tries to hand it to me, but I manage to do a pretend grab at it so that, when he lets go, it floats to the ground.

I wave goodbye as I bend down very slowly to pick it up. As he disappears, I lift the invoice with a tissue from my pocket and take it into the house, putting it on my desk in an obscure corner where I never balance my biscuits (I have a specific place where I balance my biscuits and that is precisely why).

Unfortunately, though, my paranoia doesn't end there. In fact, it is only just beginning. I notice that the cover of the septic tank that they removed won't go back very well when I try to replace it. It is corroded at one end and on the other side a piece of the edge has broken off so there is a gap, and you could lift it up if you were so inclined, which of course wouldn't matter if you didn't fiddle with it – and who would fiddle with the top of a septic tank on their weekend away in Norfolk? But then, of course, they may be the kind of family who are inquisitive, and are walking round the garden and see it, and think—

I wonder what is in there?

Mind you, you would still have to think, having lifted it up and smelt the most appalling smell this side of an open mass grave—

That's interesting! I would like to get closer to that smell.
—which is why they might lean in and fall into the septic tank, which even then is quite hard to do, because you would have to put your arms down by your sides like a torpedo to make it down into the tank, since the entrance is quite narrow. But even with all that, I immediately go to the worst and imagine the first family will arrive, drop

their bags and make straight for the septic tank, which is probably unlikely in itself, although I think at three o'clock in the morning in the week before they arrive, when I haven't slept for hours and I am completely paranoid, that that is EXACTLY what is going to happen. They are going to find the septic tank, take the cover off, make like a lot of torpedoes and then hurl themselves in. And the first review we will get for the house will be written by the local police and the courts.

So, the upshot of all this really quite reasonable/insane worrying is that I get Martin to put a heavy paving slab on top of the septic tank hole and then put the cover on the paving slab and then I think, quite reasonably, that you can still lift up the paving slab, even if it weighs a ton, despite the fact that there is no reason for lifting it in the first place, especially because, if you lift it, it smells like the worst smell you have ever smelt, even worse than a mass grave. So, given that you can still lift it, even if it takes two of you and there is absolutely no reason for you to do it, I get Martin to seal the paving stone in with special super-sticky tape that you can't peel off. He then puts the other cover on top of that.

And then I worry that you can still unpick the tape around the slab, and I imagine that a couple of young boys in particular might enjoy that challenge, and in fact it might make the septic tank even more of an attraction, so I quiz Martin about how difficult it would actually be to unpick the tape, and he is starting to get a little impatient with me now, which is surprising, as this isn't what Martin is normally like, but anyway, he tells me that this would be very difficult and would take hours and hours and you would need some sort of blowtorch or something, and even though I point out that some young boys really, REALLY like a challenge, at this point Martin is really, really, really, REALLY adamant, and actually stops smiling for a brief moment for the first time since I've met him and says that if they were going to lift off the corroded cover, peel off the tape, lift up the paving slab and dive torpedo-like into the septic tank that smells worse than a mass grave, it would probably take up their entire weekend, which, even reasonable, sensible me is forced to concede is a tiny tad unlikely.

So, I let it go.

BACK

August / September 2018

In the weeks that follow my visit to the doctor, the medication does indeed do its work. I feel different. I sleep better. There is a levelling off. I feel as if I am being supported.

Whereas before it felt as if I were a vulnerable, volatile mess, now it feels as if I am wrapped in something – protected. As if someone has their arms around me and I couldn't move even if I wanted to, which I don't.

I can still see my worries, but I am conscious now of a distance between myself and them. They are further away – smaller and less distinct. Gone are the days when they were raging right in front of me, like flames 50 feet high. And not only are they distant from me; there is, importantly, no question of my being able to bridge that divide. There is no question of my suddenly leaping back into the midst of them – that feels a physical impossibility.

In this way, the world functions. I function. I write little, if at all now. That seems like a memory. Ironically, it is the garden that keeps me going.

I have started doing more work in it – not just the regular mowing of the lawns and picking up of the leaves, but some pruning of shrubs and tending to the beds. The steady rhythm of physical labour gives me something; gives me a skeleton when it feels as if I might just collapse without it. I have no illusions about what I can accomplish. The garden overall is still a mess and will largely remain so, but that doesn't really matter right now. Just the act of being physically engaged with it seems enough.

When I do a day's gardening, I follow a strict routine, getting there at 9:30am. I will start with some hoeing, and I will concentrate on the blade of the hoe and placing it in exactly the right point to turn the weeds up. I'll feel the vibration as it sinks in all the way up the blade and the handle right through my hands, up my arms and into my shoulders. Then I will bend down, pick the weed up, shake it free of soil and throw it into the trug. I will enjoy seeing how the weeds are piling up in there – the bad, broken, negative weeds that get in the way of the peace and tranquillity of the bed.

Soon I'll feel tired and ready for a break, and that will always be roughly at 11am. And then, when I have had a cup of tea and worked some more, it will nearly be midday and my thoughts will turn to lunch, and I'll start setting myself goals. I'll say that I must have hoed to that point or that point before I'm allowed to stop. And then I'll pop home to our new house, and I'll have a sandwich, and I'll always feel dog-tired and close my eyes for ten minutes afterwards. Then a quick green tea and I'll head back to work and push on further, and for the hour after lunch it will be hard, because my body will have really slowed down and will want to sit, but I will enjoy forcing it, making it work, making it bring the hoe down again, picking up that clump of weeds, shaking the soil loose when it doesn't want to. I will enjoy taking possession of my body till after a while the voice that wants to stop fades a little, and the sun is starting to disappear, and I'll see the garden soil looking clear and dark where I've been working, and I'll feel enormously pleased that my effort has translated into results; how the plants look like they can breathe and the edges at the base of the bed are sharp, and I'll realise too how much I love the colour of the soil – the deep brown, as vivid as a deep blue or green. I will love the way the soil looks so clean and fresh and smooth. How it looks brand new. As if it has started again.

And then the day will slide downhill towards its end and I'll start to feel exhilarated at having spent so much effort and changed the picture in front of me, altered it so drastically as if I am a painter, as if I've made something.

Then there is too much to do and the day is almost over and I'll feel everything speed up and I'll take one last aim – I will finish THERE, I'll say, and I'll stop and stand, my body gently aching from my feet and ankles up through my back to my shoulders, arms and hands – every muscle in my body worked and turned and twisted and stretched.

It'll be an utterly pleasurable exhaustion. An exhaustion that feels like a present or a blessing; a buzz because I'll be all used up with nothing left to give. And it'll feel so right. As if I were designed for this.

❧

The garden is my rock, and in these weeks I am grateful for this great big hulking place. When I walk into The Valley, it feels as if I am walking into a giant bear hug. It has a strength and calm that I need. It is so steady.

Though, at my lowest, I felt the garden moving, enveloping me before my eyes, running at me, jumping on me, in many ways now the opposite feels true. Now I feel its sameness, its solidity, its rootedness. The fact it is immoveable, indefatigable. Bloody-minded.

Nothing happens fast in a garden. You look at it, then look away and back. Nothing has changed. You go back the next day, and to all intents and purposes it is still the same. The grass might grow. Leaves might fall in a week, but it is just the garden yawning, flexing its arms, then settling once again. A garden like mine is here for years, decades. The trees have been around for centuries.

So, I hold onto that strength. I draw on that. I focus on that when I arrive each day to garden.

My life is lived out a foot or two from my eyes. I don't wander, project, or fantasise. I look at that patch of bare earth in front of me and no further. I stare at it hard and concentrate. I refuse to let my mind wander.

And it's grateful in return. Just that bare patch of earth in front of it is enough. It is exhausted with all the other stuff. It wants relief. A break – from grief, from guilt, from twisting back and forth. My mind is grateful that it has somewhere to go. Some days, I don't garden at all; even the slow rhythm of the work is too much effort.

When this happens, I just sit on the garden seat that looks out from the edge of the path across The Valley. That is all I can do. I have nothing. No energy, no plans.

I find myself staring at the Gunnera in The Valley. They are remarkable, these triffid-like extraterrestrials. They are starting to wilt. They disappear to nothing in the wintertime, as if they are dead. Their stems are limp. They fall onto the ground with no strength to lift themselves. Ravaged, flat. Denuded. It is inconceivable they could recover from that state.

Yet, as spring comes, I know it will be different, because it is the same every year and I have witnessed it repeatedly. The stems regain their strength; the leaves on the end find a miraculous new shape and colour. The whole plant literally lifts itself up like a brave fighter after a heavy knockdown.

D-DAY

April 2019

As I walk round the garden on the day when the first guests arrive, literally everything appears hazardous; a deathtrap. I look longingly at the bits that Martin has roped off with 'No Entry' signs and wonder if we can do that with the whole thing.

In the maze where the firepit lives, I suddenly find the roots of various bamboo plants sticking up – so I get down on my hands and my housemaid's knee and start trying to nip them much closer to the ground. And as fast as I see one, I see another dozen. Then I realise that they could be all over this part of the garden and I see people falling all weekend – pensioners, people with sticks. What if one of them is blind and they didn't tell us? So I feel with my hand, gingerly, in large semi-circles like someone searching for landmines.

Then I notice that all the outdoor furniture is spattered with bird poo – huge dark green and brown cluster bombs, spherical and oozing, each with a jagged, hard trail. Bird poo is poisonous, isn't it? At the very least, it makes small children blind. The chair and tables in The Valley have taken a hit. The pews around the campfire are all marked. Even the swimming pool cover has been transformed overnight into an expressionist painting. It's as if the bird population has decided on one last spectacular overnight air raid – the garden's latest act of obstinacy.

And there is more, too much more.

There are the scraggy edges of the main footpath past the garage when it gets to the top of the garden, where gravel and the tired remnants of moss make a crazily shifting border – enough to send an unsteady grandpa hurtling to his death. One of the steps on the steep path down to The Valley now seems to feel soft under my feet and might cause a whole column of in-laws to concertina and fall forward like a human landslide. Branches overhead, particularly around the lawned area next to the tennis court, look as though they will drop at any moment, crushing several generations of the same family. I can almost hear the cries of "Don't move, Nana", the flash of police lights, the squeal of the ambulance. The pointing fingers. The clank of the prison gate.

Martin joins me for the last job we have time to do – a quick zoom across the top of the hedge at the front of the house, where some stray bits of foliage are poking up and spoiling the horizontal perfection of the rest. It's one of the features you will see first as you approach the drive and it's an entirely cosmetic operation, but at least it is achievable.

He sets off, standing on a ladder and clipping the tops, and I am following, just picking up the wisps and sprigs. The big sections I load straight into a trug. The thinner, wispier pieces I rake together into larger mounds and lift in handfuls. As I start, I can feel my knees ache and my back cry out every time I bend down.

Martin speeds along and I try not to get too far behind. As I work, my body gets more accustomed to the rhythm of plunging and rising. I start to feel the warmth gradually spread around the base of my spine, as if it is bound with velvet. The ache in my knees lessens too, no longer a jarring pain, more a dull pulse that merges and disappears into the other dull pulses that beat away in my very average, creaking 57-year-old body.

After a while, it is as if I can read where the branches are going to fall and I can catch them before they hit the gravel path, and the clock is literally counting down and the two of us are locked into this fantastic rhythm; the buzz of the cutters and me plunging down and then up, gloves open then closed around handfuls of foliage like salad tongs, picking them up before swinging across and dropping the handfuls into the trug. It feels as if it would be harder to break the cadence now, almost impossible, as if we can only move in this carefully choreographed dance.

In the iconic '60s movie *Cool Hand Luke* there is a scene where the convicts are shovelling sand onto a road ahead of a machine that is mixing it with bitumen to make an asphalt surface. It is hot, thankless work, a slow drudge, and they are strung out along the highway, a group of ragged individuals focussed on their own survival. Luke, suddenly inspired, speeds up his work, shovelling like a man possessed – how fast can he get to the end of the road? The others watch, and one by one are swept up by his newfound sense of purpose. They start to copy his rhythm, and what was once a series of disjointed movements becomes one whirling, energetic motion. This new energy feeds off itself. The convicts start to enjoy this human machine they've created, shovelling the sand, shouting, laughing. Faster and faster they go, and the finish line seems to sweep towards them. Then they are over it, exhausted but euphoric, smiling and sweating at the roadside, having reclaimed the task for themselves and re-found their collective spirit in the process.

When Martin has finished lopping, he shins down the ladder to help me with the last pile of foliage. Like pistons in the same engine, we duck down one after the other, lifting the leaves then putting them into the trug till the pile has disappeared from the path. We stand looking at each other for a brief minute, wiping the sweat from our brows and breathing deeply.

"Good job, Martin," I say.

"Team effort," he replies, smiling.

The first guests arrive at 4pm sharp and Emma walks them around the house and garden. I have disappeared back to the new house a quarter of an hour before, unable to cope with the moment. When Emma returns, she reports that they are a friendly family with in-laws, from North London.

"Now it's just a waiting game," she says.

❧

We spend the next day and a half sitting around our new house with Emma's phone nearby, just in case there is a problem. Emma seems able to do other things, but I can't. I read the paper but don't take it in and have to keep going back to the beginning. I misplace my glasses three times. We watch a crime thriller in the evening, but I have lost the thread of the plot by the time we are out of the first scene.

If we haven't heard anything from our visitors, is that good? Does that mean nothing is wrong? Or is it that they are so beside themselves with anger, they haven't yet found the words? Or is it because they are trapped somewhere beneath a fallen tree in the garden? Or too busy forming a human chain to get their smallest child out of the septic tank?

If there is a disaster, as by now I am convinced there must be, where will it lead? A terrible review, not just a bad one, but a brutal swingeing personal assault? And where will that take us? Other bookings cancelled, not being able to pay the mortgage, bankruptcy, the house and garden repossessed, mounting stress, tension, an end to my relationship with Emma, lawsuits, criminal proceedings, prison, homelessness, ill health, heroin addiction, a lonely painful wretched death alone in a cardboard box in a shop doorway.

I don't think I've left anything out, have I?

"Do you think they are all right?" I whisper to Emma.

It is five o'clock in the morning and she is sound asleep.

※

On Sunday at around lunchtime, Emma's phone rings and I jump like a Spitfire pilot in 1940, waiting for the order to scramble. She has asked our visitors to call her when they are about to leave.

Emma walks casually over and picks it up.

"Oh, hi there…"

It's them – must be.

"Uh-huh… Oh good!" she says into the phone.

"Good" – that's encouraging.

"Oh good…"

Another "good", although it's not "great", is it? It's still just "good".

"No, that's fine."

That's not even "good".

She rings off.

"Well?"

She walks towards me, slowly. The tension is making me desperate.

"What? What? WHAT?"

There is a pause as she inhales and stares at me, expressionless.

"They loved it!"

She shrieks and leaps on me. Totally unprepared, I grab hold of her but lose my balance and slowly pitch forwards, the two of us sinking to the floor in slow motion, like a toppled colonial statue.

"They loved everything – the house, the garden."

"Really – they loved the garden?"

"Yes."

"They didn't say anything about the untidy beds, or didn't notice the big oak bough we'd shoved into the nettles at the top of The Valley?"

"No."

"Or the leaves we'd raked under the hedges in the maze and the moss on the tennis court?"

"No."

Suddenly, the smile disappears.

"They did mention that one of the kids actually tripped and fell into…"

"Oh shit!"

The pause seems to last a lifetime.

"I'M KIDDING!"

And cool, calm Emma abandons the habits of a lifetime and turns into a mad, overexcited punk, and we pogo around the room together, crying, jumping, laughing, screaming before ending up in a sprawling, ecstatic, breathless heap on the sofa.

The review comes out on Monday, our first review, the one that will be a marker for our efforts, that all future bookers will see. It is a five-star review, though I don't remember most of what it says, but there are five words that I will never forget, words that will forever be imprinted on my heart.

"And the grounds are wonderful..."

Over the following weeks, many more people visit the house and there are other excellent reviews. New bookings flood in; a fiftieth-birthday party; a mixed hockey team; a computer company from Croydon on an away weekend; a family group from Australia researching their roots; a group of lads on the lash who leave the place so immaculate that it looks like it has been repainted.

One evening in summer we decide to look ahead and add up the total amount of money that we will make over the next six months – it is nearly £20,000. We can pay the mortgage on our new house; we can pay for the upkeep on the big house and garden. We can cover our bills for the next year or so and still have a bit extra. We are going to be all right.

We've survived and it feels as if we are more resilient for the experience; as if the bonds between us have been drawn tighter. If failure puts strain on a relationship, then success undoubtedly helps cement it.

Of course, we are too experienced and wary to think the moment is some sort of permanent panacea. All the emotional scars of the past will doubtless stay with us, but we have started making new memories again now – brighter, more optimistic and successful ones. It just feels good. And there have been so many hard, searching moments over the last ten years or so that that feeling still comes as a novelty.

It isn't quite a Hollywood ending. After all, I am still me. I still worry about small things. I am still too intense. I want things to mean other things, rather than just be themselves, and I want everything to be perfect. One event doesn't change everything, but it feels like a big event, and it surely counts for something.

❧

In the weeks and months after the first review, there is less time and opportunity to garden, and I find that I miss it. I miss the physical interaction. I miss the solid exchange of labour and result. I have forgotten the frustrations and setbacks.

I haven't become a nature obsessive yet, but if we aren't best friends, we are certainly closer than we have ever been. I still have those other passions as I did before, those 'Thinks', but something has happened to me – a door has opened onto a new and different world too, and I am curious to take a closer look.

I will never be a conventional nature lover. I will never know the names of absolutely everything in the garden. I will never be able to point out liverwort, or know when lady parsons flourish, or what you should feed a banyan tree. But nor would I want to.

I can't introduce you to my new dog now because I haven't one, I have no plans to learn a lot more onion recipes and I still hate the smell of creosote as much, if not more, than before.

But I will have a new relationship with nature because I already have. We have been through so much together. We have seen so much of each other's lives. We can't go back now – we are bonded for all time.

"Keep moving forward," said Walt Disney, and I have.

I may not know yet exactly where I have moved to, for you can never be too sure of what lies on the shady side of each peak, yet I know I am not in the same place as before.

And just the taking of that step has made me feel alive and vital, and that, for now, is enough.

❧

Posh Penny finally arrives with her family in August. She has a lovely time and leaves us wine and chocolates. After she has gone, we go to the house to prepare it for the next guests.

We find that the swimming pool filter is clogged with plastic glasses and tissues and is no longer pumping the water around the system. I find plastic glasses under the hedge and more used tissues and cotton buds scattered across the lawns. Inside the house, they haven't stripped the beds as most guests do, and they have left more tissues underneath them. Children's games have been left all over the house, sometimes with pieces missing; they have even left a chip pan full of fat outside the front door for us to get rid of. Penny and her family will prove to be, by some distance, the messiest guests we ever have.

FAREWELL

August 2020

I am saying goodbye to that view out of my bedroom window now. The view that has helped me so much.

I am standing in the spot where I sat for so many hours when I had cancer, just looking out onto the lawn, the hedge and The Valley beyond; at my favourites, the scurrying squirrels and the pigeons and the rabbits; at the light that paints the treetops and the tops of the hedges gold and frames each scene with a soft, angelic glow.

There is little in the room now – the bed has gone and the pictures have been taken down and are stacked against the walls. The sofa has been removed, the bedside tables as well, and there are two large boxes in the centre of the room marked 'Robeson Removals – Bedroom (Master)'.

I am standing with Romy and we are both looking out through that window. I have my arm around her shoulder. We've been standing there for quite some time, though neither of us could probably tell you how long.

Both of us are crying.

When the pandemic struck and the first lockdown was announced, all the bookings we had striven so hard to build up just evaporated overnight. A trickle of early emails quickly became a torrent, and people cancelled, failed to follow up initial enquiries or promised to confirm in a few weeks, then simply disappeared off the radar. In days, the business had collapsed. We were left with an empty house and no income, no way of paying the mortgage. We were like thousands of others, looking at a bleak future with nothing in the short term we could do about it.

The bigger priority was obvious. A worldwide pandemic. People dying. Severe illness. People disabled. The world literally stopping. But our own sense of emptiness was part of the story too. All that work for nothing. All that striving. And now we were back to square one – a looming financial crisis. The first phone call – "They loved it!" – so far away now, it felt like fiction rather than truth; like the soundtrack to an ancient black-and-white movie.

Because of my tortuous medical history and an immune system that still hadn't fully mended since cancer treatment, Emma and I made the decision that, with lockdown looming, I would self-isolate at the old place with Romy while Emma remained at the new house only ten minutes away with Lexy, who was still working as a receptionist at a busy hotel and, at that moment, was the most potentially problematic link in the chain.

The Thursday before it happened, I packed two suitcases, taking armfuls of hangers with clothes on them, my laptop and some TV scripts. I filled up two cardboard boxes with basic foodstuffs – tea and sugar, some bread, Marmite, pasta sauces, cheese, cold meat, tomatoes, some potatoes, chocolate biscuits and chicken soup. Everything was done in a frenzied, blurry rush. I felt like a refugee running to escape before some terrible onrushing invader.

It was strange moving back into the old house. It had an unfamiliar smell of polish and wood, like a library or a well-cleaned council building. I felt like an intruder, a burglar almost. As if I had stolen back in and it was somehow wrong. My surroundings were familiar but changed. I could see signs of my old bedroom, but much had clearly happened to it since I had used it last. There was a leather sofa in the corner I had never sat on, and the bed was a high zip-and-link one, more luxurious than before. The bedside lamps were larger and more powerful than the previous ones. The room was known to me and yet unfamiliar. We were like lovers who had been estranged and were starting again – our histories drawing us together but also keeping us apart.

By the first morning, that barrier had evaporated overnight. When I came down to have breakfast, I had moved back in time. The old familiar shapes and sounds – the curve of the banister, the creak of the stairs, the hissing of the wind through the trees outside my bedroom window – were all as they were two years ago, when it was home.

With the garden, even a brief acclimatisation was unnecessary, for any changes that had occurred since it had been a holiday let were less pronounced than inside. The paths were the same as always, the maze where Romy used to hide away was just as it was. The swimming pool and tennis court were untouched. The flowerbeds were where they had always been. The Valley was still a jaw-dropping wonderland from the pages of fiction. Even where there had been changes, they had hardly obscured the past. Where the old trampoline had disappeared along with the climbing frame, the fresh grass on the patch of earth that Martin and I had smoothed over many months before seemed to draw attention to itself and mark out the ghost of the thing it had replaced more surely than if it had been there.

Romy joined me at the house just before lockdown and we spent a blissful few weeks walking around the garden in the glorious sunshine, having tea outside, sitting and reading, playing tennis and swimming, chatting about the old days.

We talked of her mum, Vikki, a lot: the way she was, the space she made in the world, the plans she had for the house and garden, the plans she had for the family; her energy, her shyness, her integrity; the way she was good with money, a genius with decoration and absolutely useless at singing.

We talked too of how it was after she died and how we regrouped: that first party, the useless witch, the madcap dad entertainer; the parties that followed; family Christmases; the games of hide-and-seek in The Valley; new friends, new horizons, new hopes; dancing by the flames of the firepit; the way on a Sunday afternoon I used to race around the corridors in the house dragging Romy on a sled made of an open suitcase; how we used to do mock sword-fights and drag all the cushions off the sofa and the beds so that we'd have something to fall on;

how we built camps on the landing by attaching sheets to the banisters with pegs.

Sometimes we didn't talk at all. Romy would just sit on the window-ledge of her room, her legs dangling outside, and I'd be standing behind her, both of us looking silently out on that lovely view, at the fields that rolled away miles into the distance like a giant baize carpet and disappeared into the huge Norfolk sky.

We also enjoyed our time apart. Romy often lay on the kitchen lawn, reading, and I'd be sitting on a chair in The Valley, just enjoying the gentle swishing of the ferns on the banks and the graceful nods of the eucalyptus trees. As much as we'd savoured our time together, we'd always been good at giving ourselves space, just letting each other be.

It all felt like coming home in every sense – to a place, to us, a return to the simplicity of the way we were, just father and daughter, bereaved and post-bereavement, bruised but surviving and helping each other grow again in this extraordinary luxuriant space that kept the world at bay.

For two blissful months, our lives seemed to float along in this half reality, where we were living out the present but also our past life at the same time – untouched and curiously innocent, joyful and unencumbered; a strangeness in keeping with the times.

And then, as quickly as it had arrived, lockdown ended and it was as if a noisy engine had been turned on, the windows opened and a hurricane had blown in. We went from gentle isolation to noisy activity in a few, bewildering days, as Norfolk was suddenly invaded by a whole army of people who'd emerged from the confines of city life, desperate for a new start in the country.

Now we were in a desirable area, underpopulated and open with vast skies and wide beaches. Not as far from London as Cornwall, and cheaper than the home counties and the Cotswolds. Crucially, we had a three-acre garden too, a swimming pool and room for a spangly new office – room for a whole office block, in fact.

Did we want to sell?

We'd put the house on the market already two years before and it hadn't been bought, so we'd taken it off again and started the rental business. Even as recently as three months ago, we'd put it up for sale, but as a long-term backup plan and quietly, with no real expectation of getting a buyer.

Now, though, we were in a different world, with hungry cash buyers flooding out of London; houses were being snapped up in days, properties bought unseen. There was a kind of local feeding frenzy that meant, for someone like me, with a collapsing business, no income and a mortgage to pay, it was an opportunity I couldn't ignore.

Still, there was trepidation. The house and garden held so many memories for the two of us. We'd grown up there, grieved there, rebuilt there. Our DNA was in those walls, the garden paths, the trees, the shrubs. It was more than a house and garden, more than a home; it felt like a part of us – our outer skin. What would it be like when we finally let it go? How could we leave such a part of ourselves behind? Especially when we'd only recently rediscovered its joys.

❧

The first prospective buyers arrived to view the Saturday after lockdown ended, and it was obvious they weren't going to buy it. As I showed them each room, they just muttered "Uh-huh" in a monotone, as if they were at the end of a phone line and I was trying to tell them a long and involved story about how my gas meter was playing up. They marched around each room rapidly and cast bored, airy glances. The only thing that brought them to life was when we walked in the garden and they talked about whether their dog might escape from the property. They seemed very concerned about this dog getting away. They talked about fences and what the fence might be made of and how much it would cost and whether it would have gates and whether the dog might burrow underneath the fence if there was in fact a fence. Finally, when we walked back to the house, they said, "Of course, we've only just started looking at houses..." and drove away.

"They're not going to buy it," Romy said with relief when they'd gone.

When the second set of people arrived half an hour later, the feeling was different from the moment they got out of their car. They were smiling, enthusiastic, full of anticipation – two parents in their thirties with two bright-eyed children of six and nine. They glowed as if they had come home, not as if they were visiting a new one.

As they walked round the house, each room brought out new exclamations of enthusiasm and wonder. They took pictures and imagined how they would live in the space. They had already studied pictures of the house online and were thoroughly familiar with it. This first viewing felt like the second or third. They just loved it. I knew, because I recognised it; I'd seen it before, in the faces of another family 15 years previously: the same joy, the same anticipation, the same sense of belonging, the same feeling that you can identify with a place, as if it's meant to be yours.

Romy was transformed, swept up by their enthusiasm too. The silent, rather withdrawn teenager who followed me round as I toured with the first set of people was replaced by a delightful, chatty, self-possessed young woman. As I showed the mum the house, she entertained the dad and kids in the garden, kicking a football around while talking up the local school she went to, which they would be attending – tales of continuing friendship, support through difficult times, of how great it was to live five minutes away from the place when she'd forgotten her PE kit. Later, we all joined forces and walked round the garden, and she was more voluble than even I was, with her stories of hide-and-seek under the bushes, of roasting marshmallows over an open fire, of running through the maze on her sixth birthday, of the teenage gathering in The Valley she was about to have, mixing cocktails under the skies.

And this family could see it all laid out. Just as we saw it. A house and a garden to enthral, to support, to sustain and to grow up in. A place to make unforgettable memories. A place to become part of you, an outer skin.

When we'd finished and seen everything, we all ended up standing in The Valley looking around, almost in the same spot that Vikki and I had stood 15 years earlier. We stared up at the steep banks with their firs and ferns and the eucalyptus trees hanging over, casually and magnificently, almost showing off like teenage hunks on holiday and their youngest child suddenly said, "Can we just stay in the garden?"

The parents laughed and the two youngsters ran off back to the maze, and in that moment, that phrase, I knew they were going to live there.

When it was finally over and the family had departed, Romy and I walked back inside the house and shut the door.

"I hope we sell the house to those people," she said.

❧

The house is fading from our grasp now. It is becoming itself again without us – four walls, just a bare box waiting for a connection with someone else. The memories are disappearing too, each day, as the last items that held them – the furniture, the pictures, the photos, the ornaments – are packed up and leave.

We find we spend more and more time in the garden. No one can cart that off. That feels as real and connected to us as ever, perhaps more so now the house is being stripped, becoming anonymous.

Romy literally doesn't want to go inside now. She wakes up and immediately steps outside. All meals are eaten out there on the table near the hydrangeas next to the kitchen. We lie on the grass and talk or read. We ruminate. We remember hungrily, with the urgency of people who know that the clock is ticking and that those memories might soon fade.

The passage of time becomes an obsession. I find myself counting the number of occasions on which I'll still be able to cut the (almost) perfect stripes along the grass of the tennis court, or how many times I will still clear the bed near the kitchen. How many more swims in the swimming pool are left. How many times we will get to sit by the fire as dusk descends.

As the final day approaches, the dread deepens and seems to settle over us like a heavy sky. I am starting to wonder if selling the place is the right thing to do at all, even though it is a necessity. I find myself rehearsing the same arguments, even when I am alone: I must do it. I just can't afford the upkeep. Everything I have is tied up in the house and garden. I don't have a pension. I want to be able to help Romy out when she goes to college. But even though the conclusion is the same – that I must sell – it doesn't feel any better.

I try everything to soften the moment. I take a million pictures of the garden. I buy Romy a locket with a picture of myself and Mum and her in the garden. I talk to her about how lucky we have been to stay in the house in the first place, but as I say it, the words feel hollow.

I will be there till the day before the buyers arrive. Romy wants to be there till the last moment too, until the key turns in the lock for the last time. Even when the removals people come three days before completion and take away her bed, she sleeps on the floor.

※

On the last day, her aunt comes to pick Romy up – she is going to London straightaway. She doesn't want to hang around in Norfolk. We take some final, sad pictures in the front doorway and against the backdrop of the front lawn, but now we know there is nothing left to do. I give her a long hug and she leaves tearfully in the car, looking out of the rear window at the house all the way along the drive.

I finish the final clean inside, then walk round the garden one last time. There are more tears in my eyes, but I also chuckle. I see the imperfections, but now I can let them go. They will be someone else's imperfections soon.

As I walk, I see the last 15 years of my life played out in front of me in a dozen memories and I want to clutch them tightly one last time.

I see Vikki and I walking in wonderment up the path and stopping to gaze over into The Valley as we weighed up whether to buy it or not.

I see Emma when we first met, strolling up the drive with me while the kids race excitedly around us. I see myself cockily pointing ahead, strutting like a peacock in his kingdom.

I see my mum proudly looking back at the house the first time she came here with my dad. My mum, who came from a council house in London with a postage-stamp garden, lost for words as she takes in the huge green expanse, the shrubs and trees bobbing and swaying like boats on a green ocean.

I look back at my bedroom window and remember myself as the thin, exhausted patient, gazing out from the very same spot, full of envy and hope, longing to be back out there among the hedges and the shrubs, wandering free like the magnificent squirrels in the fresh, cool air.

I see this amazing, impossible, crazy, vindictive, gorgeous and plentiful space, and I want to cry because I know I shall never have anything like it again.

So much for someone who hates gardening.

❦

I put the last couple of cardboard boxes in the car and shut the boot. I am conscious of just wanting to get away. I don't want to linger. I set the burglar alarm and check that everything is switched off. Unlike Romy, I don't look back as I move off down the drive.

When I get back to our new house, I switch on the TV. It is a programme about National Trust gardens.

"We can switch it over if you like?" says Emma.

"No," I say. "Let's keep it on."

SELECTED READING

Nature Cure by Richard Mabey

An Economic History Of The English Garden
by Roderick Floud

The Salt Path by Raynor Winn

A Little History Of British Gardening by Jenny Uglow

Wild Comfort by Kathleen Dean Moore

Collected Poems by Thomas Hardy

Tess Of The d'Urbervilles by Thomas Hardy

ACKNOWLEDGEMENTS

Thanks to all the key players in the book, especially to my family and the magnificent Martin. Massive thanks also to my incredibly hardworking publicist Hannah Hargrave for her persistence and enthusiasm, Vickie Boff for her marketing genius and to Sarah Mitchell and Gail Turpin for early reading and valuable encouragement. Additional thanks to Pascale Hutton for the cover, Claire Strombeck for editing, Silke Spingies for layout, Katherine Williams and Melanie Scott for their diligent proofreading and a big shoutout to the wonderfully talented Ben Chamberlain for his incredible design input. Finally, a very special word of appreciation is due to my old friend Morwenna Banks, the original champion of this book. Without her unwavering support over several years, it would still just be a hopeful conversation over coffee in Soho.